NEW ORLEANS MEMORIES

New Orleans Memories

ONE WRITER'S CITY

Carolyn Kolb

University Press of Mississippi Jackson

www.upress.state.ms.us

The University Press of Mississippi is a member
of the Association of American University Presses.

Manufactured in the United States of America

First printing 2013
∞

Library of Congress Cataloging-in-Publication Data

Kolb, Carolyn, 1942–
New Orleans memories : one writer's city / Carolyn Kolb.
pages cm
Includes bibliographical references and index.
ISBN 978-1-61703-883-9 (cloth : alk. paper) — ISBN 978-1-61703-884-6 (ebook) 1. New Orleans (La.)—Description and travel. 2. New Orleans (La.)—Social life and customs. 3. Kolb, Carolyn, 1942-—Homes and haunts—Louisiana—New Orleans. I. Title.
F379.N54K65 2013
976.3'35—dc23 2013006724

British Library Cataloging-in-Publication Data available

TO MY FAMILY

Ken, Pherabe, Kenneth, Sarah, and Vivi

Contents

PART TWO

Mardi Gras

71

PART THREE

Literature

131

Acknowledgments

This book is a compendium of my own stories and those of many people who were kind enough to share theirs, for which I am grateful. A word of appreciation is due to Errol Laborde, of Renaissance Publishing, L.L.C., for his encouragement and for permission to use my *New Orleans* magazine columns here. I want to express my gratitude to Craig Gill, Katie Keene, Anne Stascavage, three anonymous readers, copy editor Carol Cox, and the rest of the good folks at University Press of Mississippi for their faith in me. I am also thankful to the many librarians who helped with my research at Tulane University (Leon Miller, Bruce Raeburn, Susan Tucker, Lynn Abbott, Sean Benjamin, and Ann Case); Loyola University (Art Carpenter); the University of New Orleans (Florence Jumonville); the New Orleans Public Library (Irene Wainwright); and the Historic New Orleans Collection (John Magill). And my friends who were always ready with ideas, including (but not limited to) Stuart and Olivia Bamforth, Walter Carroll, Judy LaBorde, Nell Nolan, Henri Schindler, Gasper and Mel Schiro, Constance Snow, Jack Stewart, Judy Whann, Justin Winston, Kit Wisdom, and Penny Wisdom. And, of course, thanks to my husband and to the rest of my family, who have always been an inspiration and a wonderful audience.

Introduction

Memories of New Orleans seep through a special atmosphere of the senses. In this city, even the air is different. It hangs about you, lank and sultry. When you see things through this air, they are changed in some way.

What I recall about living here, what I have seen with my eyes, heard with my ears, felt, tasted, and caught the scent of, I can pass along. And I can pass along the stories of others, because we, each of us, have our own stories, and they are precious.

I have been as truthful in this writing as I can, because I have been entrusted with stories.

When things fail, when the lights go out and the roof caves in and the water rises, all that remains, ultimately, is the story.

This work is grounded in the essays that appeared monthly as "Chronicles of Recent History" in *New Orleans* magazine. Renaissance Publishing, L.L.C., and editor and publisher Errol Laborde made all this possible. I am very grateful for this support, and for the permission to publish this work. I also thank the Louisiana Endowment for the Humanities, the magazine *Louisiana Cultural Vistas,* and Dr. Michael Sartisky, editor-in-chief, and David Johnson, editor, for publishing my essay on Frances Parkinson Keyes and allowing its use here.

In the process of writing, I pulled topics from my own memories, and I asked friends for ideas. I took suggestions from anyone willing to make one. When I was curious about something, I found experts and asked questions. Lots of questions. My family thinks I invented the ideal job for myself with those monthly essays: I get to talk to my friends, meet new people, ask nosey questions, and write whatever I want. I enjoy it immensely.

Besides conducting interviews, I did research. I hold a doctorate in urban history from the University of New Orleans, and I teach Louisiana history at Tulane University. In this writing, I did not take a scholarly approach. I don't lecture. I tell stories. And these stories are true ones. However, I also hope that teachers and students interested in New Orleans will find this book a useful tool, and perhaps it can be a fruitful source for their own work. (I have included bibliographies of books—not all of them academic—I use and enjoy.) I know that Orleanians will find many of their own memories on these pages, and yet there is so much general interest in this fascinating city that any reader will find pleasure.

The resulting writings reflect the pattern of the city. Since the devastation of Hurricane Katrina in 2005, some of these things remembered will never return. Some of the people whose stories I tell are no longer with us. It is important to me that they not be forgotten. We can honor them by sharing and enjoying their stories. Taken together, stitched into sections and connected by topics, the stories form a fabric of recollections, something we can wrap around ourselves and cherish.

I take all this personally. I am a native of New Orleans, as is my husband and both of our children. While I was born here, went to college here, and have lived here with my New Orleans husband since then, I spent the years from when I was four years old through high school in Bogalusa, Louisiana, just across Lake Pontchartrain. My father's family was in Tangipahoa Parish, also on the North Shore. But my maternal grandmother and some cousins lived in New Orleans, and the city is where we came every other weekend, and where I got my shoes, and shopped, and went out to restaurants and had adventures. I am, perhaps, that rare New Orleans native who also loves it as a tourist would: not only as a workaday home, but also as a destination with exotic appeal.

Besides providing information on a variety of New Orleans topics, this work falls loosely into the category of what journalists call "feature stories." Features are not hard news, but the same criteria should be used by the writer in producing both. You interview sources, you do research, you check facts, and you write it all as clearly as possible, while being true to your own style of expression and use of words.

New Orleans has always had an abundance of topics for features, and some fine writers have worked here in this genre: William Faulkner, Lafcadio Hearn, Lyle Saxon, Roark Bradford are among the past masters in the field, and there are numerous others.

For myself, I can only say that I am privileged to be a New Orleanian and a feature writer. I hope that my work brings you both knowledge and enjoyment.

PART ONE

Food

New Orleans has given the American palate a precious gift: a cuisine that has a universal appeal. There are so many good local recipes, and so much available as raw ingredients, that it comes as no surprise that New Orleans is a city obsessed with eating.

Beginning in the summer of 2011, Orleanians could sign up at the Crescent City Farmers Market for the annual "locavore" challenge. Could you go for a month eating only local items, things grown in the region? This is made a little easier since both sugar (from sugarcane grown and refined here) and salt (from the salt domes of Avery Island near New Iberia, Louisiana) are on the list. Yes, it is possible. And it is possible to have interesting food, fresh vegetables, seafood, dairy products, and meats. In fact, everything it takes, both to sustain life and to dine with flair, is available to Orleanians. There is a website at nolalocavore.org with details on how to participate—it is an annual event now.

I shop at the farmers' market, and I have a freezer with crabmeat, shrimp, and fish at the ready. (They say that after Hurricane Katrina the insurance adjusters had to be told that a freezer filled with seafood could indeed have great financial value: those losses were real.)

I still cook dinner every night, and a lot of my recipes start with a roux (sautéed flour, darkened and used to thicken a sauce). I am fortunate that my grandmother loved to cook and had great skill, and I still heat my oysters till their petticoats curl in her filé gumbo recipe. When I was a student at Newcomb College, once the women's college of Tulane University and now another victim of Katrina, I used to ride my bike through the neighborhoods near the dormitory in the early evening, just for that familiar smell of dinner cooking.

Actually, you can do that in just about any New Orleans neighborhood on any given day.

These essays deal with grocery stores, restaurants, and those who produce products beloved by residents. First of all, I must answer the obvious question in the minds of all older Orleanians: since my last name is Kolb, am I related to the restaurant?

Kolb's Restaurant. The front of the building has been stabilized; interior restoration is not complete. Photo by Carolyn Kolb.

Kolb's Restaurant

If you live in New Orleans and your last name is Kolb you get used to two things:

First, since everybody here pronounces the name "cob," you always have to spell it out: "That's Kolb, K-O-L-B."

And then you have to say, "Like the restaurant—but no relation."

My husband's father isn't from here, and some quick calls to various Kolb names in the New Orleans phone book turned up no relations to the Kolb's Restaurant family either.

We Orleanians have our own memories of Kolb's, which closed its doors over a decade ago. Judy LaBorde remembers her wedding, held upstairs at Kolb's, where her little sister Greta, aged about four, entertained guests by singing from atop an upright piano. I, myself, remember the Wiener schnitzel and the red cabbage. I recall fondly the turtle soup. And you can duplicate one of my favorite menu items, Kolb's house dressing: mix one cup Creole mustard, one-quarter cup tarragon vinegar, one-quarter cup salad oil, one tablespoon sugar, one-quarter cup water, and two tablespoons lemon juice (the *Times-Picayune*'s website published this).

Kolb's was a German restaurant, but with a decided Creole flavor. Red beans and rice was a menu stalwart. It was popular with people who worked downtown, in the days when major offices were always downtown. You could even get into the restaurant via the back alley and stroll through the kitchen on the way to your table, maybe with a quick glance at the stove to see what looked good.

Perhaps the most memorable thing about Kolb's German décor was the grill area with its intricate system of pulleys and ceiling fans attached to a little figure in lederhosen who seemed to run the fans by turning a crank. It was such a remarkable sight that I could never bring myself to eat anything in the room with those fans—do you chew in time to the lederhosen guy, whose name was supposedly Ludwig—or do you follow the fans with your eyes? It was all too dizzying for me. The apparatus with its fans and figure was said to have come from the 1884 Cotton Centennial Exposition in Audubon Park—no doubt it was a wonder of the fair.

Kolb's Restaurant dated from 1899 and was founded by Conrad Kolb, German immigrant and eager entrepreneur. The building on St. Charles Street (it's "street" in the business district and "avenue" above Lee Circle) where Conrad put his restaurant already had an interesting history.

Daniel Pratt came to New Orleans from Georgia in 1846 and built the St. Charles property, three stories, brick, with balconies, for the storage and sale of his cotton gins. By the 1850s, the address also boasted a third-floor art gallery where exhibitions of local and traveling artists' work were held. Then, for some years, the Louisiana Jockey Club operated there, and, no doubt, this racy past made it attractive as a location for Conrad Kolb's establishment when it opened late in the century. In 1981 the building (actually there are two adjoined buildings facing St. Charles) was declared a National Historic Landmark.

When Kolb's Restaurant opened, there was a thriving German culture in New Orleans—German newspapers, German singing societies, German Protestant churches, German Catholic churches—but with World War I and anti-German feeling, New Orleans's German culture went into the background.

Betsy (Mrs. Andreas) Reising, whose late husband was a cousin of the Kolb family and owner of the restaurant for a period after 1954, remembered hearing that, during World War I, Conrad Kolb had been hanged in effigy on Canal Street. Happily, that wartime antagonism did not last, and Kolb's Restaurant was soon popular enough to become the site of early meetings of the newly formed Kiwanis Club, 180 members strong in 1919.

Kolb's also became a landmark in the early history of jazz. In fact, Kolb's was one of the first respectable establishments to offer jazz music, according to material at Tulane University's William Ransom Hogan Jazz Archive of New Orleans. One of those early jazz events was re-created in May of 1983 when Tulane's "Hot Jazz Classic" included a concert at Kolb's with legendary jazzman Johnny DeDroit leading the

Louisiana Repertory Jazz Ensemble. Back in 1919, DeDroit and his band played regularly at Kolb's for dances and quickly became known for their infectious, danceable rhythms. DeDroit died in 1986 at the age of ninety-three. Today, a jazz-themed walking tour brochure put out by the New Orleans Jazz Historical Park includes a stop at Kolb's location. Sadly, what you find there now is only the old neon sign and the façade and balconies: the inside has been gutted.

It has been half a century since any Kolbs were associated with the building. Among the few local reminders of the family is a Kolb niece still in town, and carrying on the name are a Kolb great-nephew and his son in St. Tammany Parish. Conrad Kolb's extensive stein collection has been spread among family members and collectors.

Even the Kolb farm, which stood until the second half of the twentieth century as a charming Victorian farmhouse on fenced property just above the Industrial Canal, was razed for the former Schwegmann grocery store next to it and became part of their parking lot and warehouse area, Mrs. Reising noted. Her sister-in-law, Gertrude Reising Melun, lived in Georgia, but fondly remembered Conrad and Mamie Kolb, the house they lived in on St. Charles near Broadway, their farm in Gentilly with its gardens and sunroom, happy days she spent watching Mardi Gras parades from Kolb's balcony, and courting her husband at Saturday "Tyrolean Night" parties.

Kolb's Restaurant, long out of the family, finally closed, and in November 1994, the building's contents were auctioned. (We managed to acquire four small beer glasses emblazoned with a Kolb crest.) The property somehow became part of a parcel with the old Whitney City Bank branch building at 124 Carondelet Street (now also only a shell) and various corporate owners promised grand hotel projects.

Since the Kolb site was declared a National Historic Landmark and the interior portion was gutted under a former owner, the local Historic District Landmarks Commission held an escrow account amounting to $540,000 in 2002. Those funds were released to restore the façades on St. Charles and Carondelet. But, as of now, the interior of Kolb's still has not been restored.

Ludwig and the fans might be gone, but most Orleanians would be glad to raise a glass to a restored Kolb's—even if it's only the original building front that remains.

Off the Menu

LIKE MOST ORLEANIANS I tend to obsess about food—it is no surprise that when my husband and I go out to eat, just the two of us or with others, we usually spend a lot of time at the table talking about other places we've eaten. Try this: next time you eat out in New Orleans, be quiet a minute and listen to the other tables—besides laughter (people around here laugh a lot more in restaurants than they do in other towns) I guarantee you will catch snatches of restaurant reviews or recipes.

Even when the restaurants or the dishes are no longer around, that doesn't mean they vanish from memory and conversation. And people still have strong opinions about them.

There's a spot at the end of the television interview show *Inside the Actor's Studio* when the visiting star is asked: "What do you hope will be said to you when you arrive in heaven?"

I have my answer ready: "Galatoire's does our room service, the pompano are running, and Princess Cup is back on the menu!"

Suffice it to say, pompano—just broiled, with butter—is my favorite Galatoire entrée.

Princess Cup—that concoction of canned fruit cocktail over vanilla ice cream with a hearty dose of a liqueur (Grand Marnier, I think)—was my most favorite childhood dessert. But, to my chagrin, I can no longer enjoy it. It's OFF THE MENU.

As proved by Marcel Proust with his madeleine crumbs in the tea, there are certain tastes that bring back special memories, and there are certain dishes that we recall fondly but can no longer savor.

What about those yummy, soggy chicken tacos that Popeyes used to sell? That was a special dish. Now, granted, Popeyes's main offering—their variety of fried chicken—is not exactly like the version

Off the menu: Galatoire's 1940s menu, Princess Cup in dessert section, Southern Food and Beverage Museum. Note that "If Available" is stamped on the menu, likely reflecting wartime rationing. Photo by Carolyn Kolb.

once available at Jim's Fried Chicken on Carrollton Avenue. Remember how Jim's always packed it with a dill pickle slice on top?

Since Orleanians' favorite table talk always concerns food, I venture to say that conversation through a multicourse banquet could be devoted to the menu offerings at the former D. H. Holmes Restaurant on Canal Street. Oh, the liver and onions. The redfish court bouillon—always served with big canned green peas. Then, there was the fried trout with tartar sauce. And we haven't even begun to reminisce about the candy counter.

Some folks might even miss the big scale that used to stand outside the Holmes Restaurant—where you could weigh in front of a crowd if you so desired.

Another lost menu item is in the price category—as charming as the new, spruced-up Arnaud's is, some of us still long for its musty former guise when there was a $1.85 table d'hôte offering of shrimp Arnaud, followed by heart of lettuce salad, trout meuniére with Brabant potatoes, cup custard and a *'tit noir* of coffee for dessert.

Who could forget all the strange philosophical slogans adorning the walls of Wise's Cafeteria? The eggplant casserole was so heavenly one could never remember reading anything. I had lunch with a film crew at Wise's once and a cameraman ate five desserts and told me he had covered the major food groups (this is the sort of thing cameramen are wont to do).

The cafeteria star in my personal galaxy has to be reserved for Morrison's—the downtown one with the Spanish décor. There you were, under the painted stars in the ersatz patio, surrounded by the intriguingly lit balconied windows, patiently standing in line under the pretend-adobe arch inscribed "Vinos Finos De Mesa." But where else would you find baked mackerel with butter, paprika, and lemon juice? Not to mention the perfectly fried shrimp. And there was a nice waiter to carry your tray, too.

One of the most poignant losses in the restaurant roster is Chez Hélène. Even if the television show *Frank's Place* enshrined it in our memories, Chez Hélène is still missed. The cornbread. The stuffed peppers. The potato salad. Happily, the *Tremé* television series takes restaurants just as seriously as *Frank's Place* did, and the late Austin Leslie's fried chicken recipe, prize of Chez Hélène's menu, is very close to the one you can eat at Jacques-Imo's on Oak Street.

A food that was always associated with special events was Turkey Poulette at the Blue Room of the Roosevelt Hotel. It was an open-faced turkey sandwich, heavy on the sauce. Probably it was the least expensive item on the menu—but that did not detract from its charms. What else would you want to eat while watching an ice-skating show on a miniature rink at a Sunday afternoon birthday party? We once heard Bette Midler, with Barry Manilow accompanying her on the piano, while we munched our Turkey Poulettes.

Another special-event food—a ladies' luncheon, a big date—was the oyster and artichoke casserole at Corinne Dunbar's. And where else would you get a big slice of fresh pineapple? Corinne Dunbar's, with its dinner-at-a-nice-house atmosphere, was a place for very special occasions.

When meals were really inexpensive—Buster Holmes could feed you for less than a quarter—people could regularly go to sit-down restaurants and enjoy lots of courses. Stephen and Martin's—where Jo Ann Clevenger's Upperline Restaurant is now—had inexpensive weekday dinners that included soup, salad, entrée, and dessert; they made a good turtle soup, too. There was a businessman's lunch at the St. Charles Hotel that my late friend Betty Wisdom remembered with fondness, especially the red beans and rice.

Ben Abadie's Café always had a good business crowd downtown—one of their homey offerings was a lunch of knackwurst, potatoes, and sauerkraut. It was the sort of restaurant that had a dark carved bar, a floor of tiny octagonal tiles, and some framed pictures with bright blue names and slogans fashioned from butterfly wings. There was a score of such places across the city.

And then there are the vanished exotica—what about the Fog Cutter drink at the Bali Ha'i? It was sweet, full of rum, and it came in a ceramic cup shaped like an Easter Island statue. Instant sophistication.

I think I once tasted snapper throats at the Beaconette, where that was the signature dish. The Black Orchid, upstairs on Foy Street in Gentilly, always put a thin slice of fresh peach in your wine glass. Fried parsley was always served in a basket when you took your table at Maurice Bitoun's restaurant on the West Bank. A place called Triangle Seafood off Leake Avenue made the best hard-crab salad—it was more like marinated crab claws. The hard-boiled egg remoulade course at Maylie's might even fit in the exotic category (since I have a friend who still makes that remoulade recipe we get to have the dish at home now).

There were special restaurants for times of the day. Allgood Restaurant next to Touro was open round the clock—if you had a hankering for cheese or applesauce blintzes at 3 a.m. they could accommodate you, and their hamburgers were legendary. When the Morning Call was at the other end of the French Market it was the after-party place to go, with its powdered-sugar shakers chained to the counter.

And there were personalities at certain restaurants that are no longer there—Sal and Maria at Compagno's on St. Charles (oh, their spinach was soooo good—and it wasn't even a specialty), Rose and her sister at the old-time Delmonico's (with Delmonico fluff for dessert and that marvelous mural over the bar).

In these days with personality chefs and fusion cooking and constantly changing menus, the restaurants and recipes of the past may seem a little too simple, a bit trite. But one can still miss a good dish when it disappears.

And, in point of fact, whatever happened to that weird Sauce Alciatore at Antoine's—the one that was like a béarnaise sauce with a little pineapple juice added? I know it was on that menu just a while ago . . .

Solari's

Besides eating in restaurants, Orleanians have always eaten well at home. New Orleans recipes, the classic ones, rely on simple, local ingredients. Some of them, even in the city, you could find in the backyard: gardens had herbs and vegetables like tomatoes and peppers and mirlitons (chayotes). Trees could yield bay leaves, pecans, oranges, and even alligator pears (avocados). With the ingredients and the kitchen skills, you can keep a New Orleans kitchen wherever you are. Obviously, not everything can be found around the house. You had to go to market, and in New Orleans, even that could be an adventure.

Before New Orleans had any supermarkets, shopping was a vastly different experience. In the past, some venders even came to your house. We had an egg man, and we even had a vegetable man until my neighbor backed into his van, and I was once in a group that regularly had deliveries of a five-gallon tin of freshly shucked oysters that we split.

There are truck vendors parked at regular locations: one is on South Carrollton right in front of the Catholic Notre Dame Seminary. The trucks might cruise through neighborhoods, and even today there is a "Mr. Okra" with a fancifully painted truck and a singsong line of patter he broadcasts to bystanders.

Shopping in the pre-supermarket days involved visiting one of the big public markets, the biggest and best known being the French Market across from Jackson Square. There were other public market buildings, some of which I can remember in use. The one on St. Roch Avenue at St. Claude Avenue held an amazing seafood market, where you could actually buy a live turtle.

However, Orleanians always wanted a little something fancier, and

Solari's, "Where Quality Reigns Supreme." Courtesy of Louisiana Division/City Archives, New Orleans Public Library.

when it came to groceries, the preferred fancy vendor for many years was Solari's.

Long before there was a Whole Foods Market, New Orleanians had a favorite pricey store where they could find out-of-the-ordinary grocery items, fresh vegetables and meats, prepared cooked dishes, a lunch counter, exotic ingredients, freshly made pastries and candies, and—best of all—they delivered.

From 1863 to 1961 Solari's, which occupied the spot where Mr. B's Restaurant is now, was synonymous with good eating in New Orleans—even the *New Yorker* magazine once noted, "If you like poking around in stores, try Solari's at Royal and Iberville Streets, a grocery like none other in the world."

When the founder, John B. Solari, died in 1891, his obituary recorded that he was born in Genoa, Italy, in 1819, and came to America as a young man, first settling in Plaquemine, Louisiana. He moved to New

Orleans, opened his store in 1863, and operated it with his son, A. M. Solari, who died suddenly the year before his father. The remaining family carried the business into the twentieth century.

Solari may have opened his business while the city was occupied with the Civil War, but he quickly demonstrated his showmanship in cornering the fine food market while being in the technological forefront of the times. An 1877 story in the *Times-Democrat* newspaper detailed how telephone wires were strung between the original location on Camp Street and Solari's new main store on Royal Street. The first phone call concerning overnight orders merited front-page coverage.

Those on hand for the occasion, besides the press, included both Dr. Armand Mercier, president of the Athenaeum (a studious local group) and the local sales representative for Piper Heidsieck champagne. When the phone was hung up, Solari entertained his guests, including the press, by serving "a splendid collation" with the host displaying his flair as a "man of the world."

Having your groceries delivered from Solari's was not only a sign of your good taste; the delivery itself was an event. One New Orleans matron, who grew up in her grandmother's home on Esplanade, fondly remembers the Solari's delivery coach—"It was a wagon, but so black and shining." As a special treat, "I was always allowed to pet the horse," she recalled. Besides foodstuffs and sundries, her grandmother always ordered bottled water from Solari's. "It came in long, thin, tall bottles. I can see it to this day. It was always sent upstairs to her room," she said.

Another Louisiana lady remembers that her father, who was French, always had a special fondness for Solari's. "He could get real Roquefort cheese there, not just blue cheese. And he always ordered guava jelly—it came in a little wooden box."

For years Orleanians anticipated the new edition of the Solari's catalog—which warned that "all purchases will be billed at the prevailing price when ordering." In 1931, the variety of foods was astounding.

The bakery department was staffed by "trained women bakers who patiently 'fuss' over each cake to get it just the way it should be," and their offerings included layer cakes with orange or lemon custard fillings, caramel cakes, maple pecan cakes, jelly cakes, devil's food cakes, and a number of other types.

The candy department, besides having pralines and decorated mints, offered chocolates, of which the "Solari's Assortment, $1.25 the pound may consist of all assorted chocolates, or chocolates and bonbons or all bonbons." There were marzipan sweets in strange shapes—elephants, violins, or even watches. There were decorated sugar cubes for afternoon tea.

Under the heading of foie gras there were seventeen items listed (plus two foie gras mousse varieties.) There were thirty-two different imported cheese items, plus domestic cheeses. Cooked foods included gumbos, jambalaya, roasted spring chickens, stuffed crabs, and almost anything else to grace a dinner table. There were innumerable sausages and preserved meats, plus groceries and canned goods of all kinds, kitchen sundries, a long list of breakfast foods, and a health food section.

Solari's made their own mayonnaise fresh every morning, and there were seventy-five different sandwiches on their lunch counter menu—a club sandwich at fifty cents being the most expensive, with roast beef listed at fifteen cents.

Besides Solari's wines, spirits, and a large selection of bitters, in the early 1930s there were still long lists of cordial syrups (nonalcoholic), which were used for flavoring your own concoctions in prohibition days. An Internet search even found someone seeking a value for "two Monopoles Alfred Rothschild wines . . . Brut 1953 and Rose Brut 1955 . . . a label on the bottles says 'Exclusively at Solari's of New Orleans.'"

Solari's kitchen was even good enough so that Chef Warren LeRuth, when he decided to quit L.S.U. and devote himself to cooking, apprenticed at Solari's in the 1940s.

Many Orleanians retain memories of the famed Solari's lunch counter. William Faulkner apparently liked his lunch so much that he left barefoot, forgetting his shoes under the counter stool. One local businessman recalls, "We always had a sandwich—it was good delicatessen. I would get corned beef." But it was the smell of the pickle barrels that everyone immediately recalls.

One Orleanian, who recalls lunching with her mother when she was a child, noted that "I remember the pickle barrels—I was allowed to take a pickle home one time. And I don't think I ever in my life saw another cracker barrel, but they had one at Solari's."

Going downtown to shop often included a Solari's lunch. "I always had to wear a nice dress, socks, shoes, and Mother always had a hat," she remembered. "Solari's was this big, huge place it seemed to me, with everything in the world in it."

What she remembered most about the lunch counter was the sign hanging over it, warning, "No Reading at the Counter Between 12 and 1." "I was always allowed to read at meals, but I knew they did not want you to stay too long during lunch."

Even picky little girls liked their food at Solari's. "I especially liked their squash, and I could always eat Solari's food. My mother liked their collard greens. And I could get a cookie for dessert." Other fond lunch memories included the half-avocado salad with crabmeat.

Solari's closed in 1961, and, despite a brief resurrection as a delicatessen, it quickly morphed into a parking garage until the opening of Mr. B's by the Brennan family restored part of the original building to culinary uses.

When Solari's closed there was a grand going-out-of-business sale. A man who was then an employee of the Louisiana State Museum remembered he bought a bottle of Goldwasser liqueur. "It tasted like licorice, but I liked the idea of the flecks of gold in it." Some Newcomb students splurged on white Chianti in baskets. The prices were low and the selection was eclectic. And, too soon, it was over.

While it is nice to have stores that offer prepared foods, and even a place to sit and eat, there are those who miss the days when you could dial MAIN 8500 and the Solari's delivery man would bring you a daube glacé, a pot of gumbo, and a jelly cake.

Grocery Memories

SITTING AT THE COMPUTER and using the Internet to "make groceries" is possibly the most joy-killing use of technology since the admission of cell phones to restaurants.

There has always been something special, almost sacred, about the task of stocking a New Orleans larder. It's more than just shopping. Even today, going to market is a ceremony celebrating life, not a mundane chore. Fond remembrance of past shopping experiences is something that haunts us all, even today.

Granted, somewhere back in the long-distant past I can recall the beautifully arrayed vegetables at "N. Lala Stall No. 14" in the French Market, and I have an equally fuzzy memory of caged chickens at some long-ago venue my grandmother frequented. But you need not go far back in the past for grocery memories that you'd have to work hard to re-create today. Historian Sally Reeves once gave a talk on New Orleans grocery history that was highlighted by her recollections of going home for lunch while she was a Newcomb student, and having a menu made up of fresh fruits, vegetables, meat, and seafood—even tiny, pink river shrimp—entirely fresh, locally produced, and all delivered by the stalwarts employed by Miss Lucy at Vonderhaar's Grocery on Magazine Street, now the very trendy La Petite Grocery restaurant.

Grocery memories can include those dim interiors of the Hill Stores that once dotted New Orleans corners. And, although there are at least two Piggly Wigglys left on the West Bank, that first of all southern supermarket chains used to have addresses all over town. The one on St. Charles near Napoleon was such a nice place—even when little children in their strollers would knock all the mayonnaise jars off the bottom shelf the Piggly Wiggly folks just smiled and wiped up.

Grocery memories: Piggly Wiggly Grocery Store, Westwego, Louisiana. Photo by Carolyn Kolb.

Another chain that used to be dotted around the neighborhoods, Canal Villere, somehow morphed into National and then begat the SuperStore—the first grocery I can recall that, for a while at least, wanted you to pack things in cardboard boxes instead of bags, the way Sam's Club does now. When the SuperStore opened on Tchoupitoulas Street, the butcher's department had a selection of very odd meats, including venison and buffalo. New Orleans cooks are inventive, and certainly are used to trying to cook anything shot by a household member, but the meat counter zoo selection soon disappeared for lack of customer interest.

If there were an award for most-missed grocery chain in New Orleans, the hands-down winner would be the Schwegmann's Supermarkets. Back to the giant quonset hut store on Airline Highway, Schwegmann somehow claimed a quirky place in the hearts of local shoppers. Yes, the prices were low—and remember, it was the late

John Schwegmann, Sr.'s suit that bolstered consumers' rights and lowered milk prices. (And it went all the way to the U.S. Supreme Court, where he won.)

John Schwegmann was such a larger-than-life figure it was not surprising that he ran for governor (and lost) and served in the legislature. When he went to Europe, he would write about his travels and put his letters right in his grocery ads. For years it was a prized political endorsement if a candidate's face adorned a Schwegmann bag. (And the Schwegmann's baggers were always winning speed prizes so those bag/ads moved quickly around.)

It was said that many immigrant groups found their first jobs as Schwegmann checkout clerks, and supposedly the store on Veterans just above Causeway was the training location. Was this true? It doesn't matter, really, because it was a good story and it fit with the local involvement the Schwegmann's stores were famed for. After all, these were stores that provided customers with a bar so they could have a beer and a poor boy while they cruised the aisles. In-house liquor brands like Old Piety and Burgundy were stocked at Schwegmann's, along with an incredible variety of other goods—in a day when big chains were limiting their items on the shelves, Schwegmann's seemed bent on proving that no product was too obscure to stock. And, since they had a little of everything, everyone had to go there at least once.

Crowds at Schwegmann's were rather like crowds at Carnival parades—you were inclined to get into conversations with all manner of people simply because you were standing next to them. I recall buying some squid because I was going to try fried calamari, and I gathered a crowd of curious shoppers wanting to know how I planned to cook them. Schwegmann's always stocked the turkey necks near the seafood because they can be a major gumbo ingredient—and only real New Orleans stores would remember that.

Each Schwegmann store seemed to have its own personality. The big one near the Industrial Canal had a large stock of fishing equipment for those bound across the lake (and supposedly they used to stock one-hundred-pound sacks of sugar for Mississippi moonshine makers when that was a dry state). The Gentilly Schwegmann's also had a good cheese department, at a time when, at least in some households, anything other than rat cheese was adventuresome. At the Annunciation Street store and the one on North Broad, you could park on the roof (there have been occasional drive-in movies on the roof of the North Broad building while it was vacant). The Airline Highway store seemed to have the most extra departments—a barbershop, for instance, not to mention the Schwegmann's Bank.

Schwegmann's, of course, has gone—maybe there is a celestial mall where Schwegmann's went (right next to a K&B, of course). However, Rouse's, a Louisiana chain begun around Bayou Lafourche, has expanded rapidly and quickly won the hearts of residents with local products and endorsements from major local chefs, plus a seafood department stocked with local catch and a dependable cooked-food area.

We are fortunate in New Orleans that there are still neighborhood groceries where shopping is more than a dull check-off-the-list experience.

Can many regulars get through Langenstein's without at least one long conversation? I fondly recall a heated discussion about school board candidates next to the onion bins. And who has not walked sideways through at least one aisle at Dorignac's? If they gave a prize for number-of-products-per-aisle, Dorignac's would win, and shopping there is still a fun experience even if Mr. Joe is no longer seated in the front with his racing form checking his winners. Plus, they play old rock-and-roll hits on their sound system.

Robert's (pronounced, of course, ro-BAIRS) has claimed its Lakeview niche on Robert E. Lee and branched out to Metairie and Carrollton, and they pay attention to local recipes when stocking their shelves.

All the farmers' markets have kept local cooks happy with fresh ingredients and have cut down on mileage to Plaquemines for oranges or up to Hammond for strawberries—now they come to town! We may miss the delivery boy from Saladino's, on Garfield near State Street, who could even bring you a homemade sandwich with your order, but there are still small stores like Zara's, uptown and in the lower Garden District, that prepare their own dishes for sale besides having the pantry items.

Orleanians will always have favorite stores, and wise storekeepers are going to keep trying to meet New Orleans tastes. Happily, there are still spots where you don't always have to "make groceries" in a sterile giant box, and where there is still someone in a white apron behind the butcher counter who can cut you a thick steak or find you a veal pocket.

After all, it's what happens to those ingredients back home in your kitchen that matters most.

Leidenheimer

May 2006

Orleanians know that there is one culinary staple our local cuisine requires: French bread. And it has to be the kind with the crispy crust and the light interior, the kind you can squash down on a poor boy, or hollow out for an oyster loaf, the kind that soaks up the butter and garlic until it turns ooze-ie yellow when you make garlic bread.

We might say French bread, and there are other bakeries, but mostly we mean Leidenheimer's. Their trucks are emblazoned with the Vic and Nat'ly cartoons of Bunny Matthews, and their long poor boy loaves in paper wrappers are found sticking out of shopping bags in an amazing number of places.

Just how necessary Leidenheimer's bread was became obvious after Hurricane Katrina.

When you're running a top, hot new restaurant in Washington, D.C., you have to be prepared for any and all emergencies if you want to keep satisfying your customers. Jeff Tunks, master chef presiding over the kitchen of the trendy Acadiana Restaurant in the nation's capital, had honed his skills at the Culinary Institute of America, and, after a stint as head chef at the Grill Room of the Windsor Court in New Orleans, was ready to teach the world a thing or two about Louisiana food. Acadiana was packed every night, and Tunks's ears were burning with compliments. He prided himself on his authentic bayou state ingredients. On his menu, among various Creole and Cajun specialties, was his popular offering "The Peacemaker"—none other than a New Orleans oyster loaf. And Tunks liked to serve bread from New Orleans's own Leidenheimer Bakery. The real thing.

Then came Hurricane Katrina.

Leidenheimer Baking Company workers. Photo courtesy of Leidenheimer Baking Company.

The nation watched mesmerized, as day followed day and tragedy heaped on tragedy. Suffering was universal. In Washington, Chef Tunks was in despair. Much of New Orleans was under water and, to add to his misery, Leidenheimer itself was not operating. How could he serve anything but the finest, lightest, crustiest loaf of New Orleans bread?

Naturally, Leidenheimer came to his rescue. If they couldn't bake in New Orleans, they'd find someplace dry to do it.

As Sandy Whann, the fourth generation of the family operating Leidenheimer, explained, "Within a week of the storm hitting, we had been in touch with our friends around the country who are in the baking business. We arranged for our operations manager to travel to Chicago and produce our product in a friend's bakery." Even the muffuletta loaves came out of the Chicago ovens ready for olive salad and cold cuts.

You can't keep a good bakery down. As soon as its Simon Bolivar Avenue location had dried out, Whann had the ovens heated and running. Over a hundred years of food perfection can't be sidelined easily.

The bakery's founder, George Leidenheimer, arrived in the city from Deidesheim, Germany, in 1896. His bakery started on Dryades Street, but by 1904 it was in its present location. Early loaves were probably dense, dark, German breads. But a good baker looks for ways to please his customers. As Whann explained, "Our bread is probably a combination of the early German baking heritage combined with the food we have in south Louisiana."

Whann sees seafood as the key: "As seafood was so accessible, our bread matched that seafood." Leidenheimer loaves are designed "to complement what is on the sandwich rather than take it over." The "traditional New Orleans French bread" comes in all sizes, from long poor boys to pistolettes.

But is New Orleans French bread really French? Could you get it in Paris? Whann has an opinion on that, too. "Actually, there's not much difference." That is because "many different types of bread are found in Paris. It varies block by block—in terms of its lightness and thinness of crust." Whann also believes that "what typically passes off in the United States as a Parisian baguette doesn't resemble that found in Paris: it's too doughy, the crust is too chewy." New Orleans French bread, as Whann bakes it, hits all the high notes of crisp crust and light interior.

Leidenheimer's has a long, proud history and a hopeful future. Sandy, otherwise known as Robert J. Whann IV, was honored in 2002 as a "Rising Star" of the baking industry. According to trade publication *Baking and Snack*, his "devotion, dedication and determination" combined with "energy, passion and vigor" earned him accolades for a career spent running his family business. Starting by bouncing on flour sacks as a child, he earned a degree in business administration at Virginia's Washington and Lee University, while working in various bakeries during vacations. Finally, he came into Leidenheimer, where his sister, Katherine Whann, is office manager.

Their father, Robert J. Whann III, had taken over the bakery operation as a young man on the sudden death of his father, and mutual family respect has gone a long way toward keeping the operation running smoothly as, metaphorically speaking, the baker's hat passed from one head to another.

Running a bakery involves more than mixing dough. Sandy Whann admits to keeping a close eye on the commodity market. "It's a key aspect of our business," he admits.

And baking bread calls for huge quantities of wheat. "We have folks we work with at Horizon Milling, just outside of Baton Rouge. We use a very high quality flour, with high gluten content. Our wheat comes from the Dakotas, Kansas, and Minnesota. Sometimes we use all spring wheat, sometimes a spring and winter blend. We change the type of flour we use based on what the year's crop is like," Whann explained.

Sandy Whann has also expanded the business as times have changed. Bread is shipped frozen around the country, with Texas being an especially good market. Since the early 1990s, Leidenheimer's has owned Reisings Bakery, and prior to Hurricane Katrina, purchased Angelo Gendusa's Bakery.

Whann's restaurant customers, from grand establishments here and elsewhere to the humblest poor boy stand, are the driving force of the bakery. Citing the "creativity of our chefs," Whann had high praise for new innovative takes on traditional New Orleans food. In fact, Whann joined with local chef Susan Spicer in founding Wild Flour Breads, producing "hand made artisan bread, old world Italian breads, and some French breads."

Leidenheimer maintains a quiet presence in the city, but one longtime commercial jingle still is remembered. As Sandy Whann explained, "We actually had some television commercials when I was a child—I even appeared in them." The song dates from the commercial, gaining brand loyalty with the lyrics "Ooh la Leidenheimer. That's what I said. Ooh la Leidenheimer. That's fresh for bread." (Or, in another version, "That's fresh for French bread.") Even though "we're neck and neck with Rosenberg's" in the nostalgic commercial song derby, Leidenheimer's tune today is heard only on hold on the company telephone line.

While he is "incredibly proud of what our employees have done," there was a lot of work to be done post-Katrina. One thing that annoyed him was the replacement fleet of plain white trucks. Sure enough, Bunny Matthews's quintessentially New Orleans "Vic 'N Nat'ly" drawings are back.

Whann has decided opinions on how his bread is treated best. "Never microwave it. That's for popcorn, not bread," he cautions. "Whatever you don't use, freeze it that day." Whann also warned, "Never thaw bread, all you do is aid the staling process. Put it right into the oven frozen." As his personal favorite way to eat Leidenheimer's bread, Whann recommends toasting a loaf of poor boy bread in a 350 degree oven. Butter it well, and fill the sandwich with any fried seafood you choose. "And that's followed closely by the perfect hot roast beef.

"Fortunately there are a lot of our hardworking customers out there who are making lots of those," Whann noted proudly.

Montalbano's: Home of the Roma Sandwich

THE MUFFULETTA is the other iconic New Orleans sandwich—and Leidenheimer makes a bread for this one, too. The muffuletta also represents another culinary ancestor of New Orleans cuisine: Italy (more properly, Sicily). Today most Orleanians have spaghetti and red gravy with meatballs as a normal family meal, proof that Italian cooking has had a lasting impact on New Orleans tables.

One of my own favorite food memories involves the muffuletta. When I was very young, my father took my mother and me to a small shop deep in the French Quarter to get one of these sandwiches.

What a ceremony it was: before our eyes, the sandwich was created on half a loaf of round bread, while my father chose the ingredients from the glass cases of delicatessen items. Wrapped in butcher paper, this wheel of a sandwich was presented to us. The three of us barely made a dent in it and we took it home in all its garlicky glory.

Although nowadays I am happy to line up for a spectacular sandwich at Central Grocery Company on Decatur Street, I consider myself fortunate to have had a personal encounter with Mr. Montalbano, a pioneering practitioner of the muffuletta art.

Biaggio Montalbano was a passionate man. He was devoutly religious and practiced his religion publicly. And he was equally devoted to food, serving, preparing, and selling a remarkable sandwich on round Italian bread, the loaf shape carrying the name muffuletta. He called his version of that garlic-enhanced concoction of olive salad, meats, and cheeses the "Roma Sandwich." From his domain at 724 St. Philip Street, Mr. Montalbano reigned supreme for decades, a devoted and eccentric purveyor of one of Sicily's best gifts to New Orleans.

Beginning in the years before World War I, the French Quarter was home to numerous Italian, and, more particularly, Sicilian immi-

Central Grocery Company, 923 Decatur Street—where to get your muffuletta today, now that Montalbano's is closed. Photo by Carolyn Kolb.

grant families. Fruits, vegetables, groceries—these were the products that provided the livelihood for many of these Orleanians. The great international fruit companies would grow from this beginning, and so would countless family-run groceries and restaurants.

In 1917, the Montalbano brothers—listed on the deed as Biaggio, Calogero, and Sebastian—purchased a small house on a long narrow lot at 724 St. Philip Street from a widow, Virginia Schiro Marciante. The Montalbanos, according to obituary details, originally came from Contessa Entellina, Sicily. Many New Orleans families came from this small Sicilian town, most of whose residents were actually descendants of ethnic Albanians, the "Arberesh." Biaggio would marry Mary Sciambra, and the Sciambra family members were also owners of 724 St. Philip.

A front room of the house soon became a delicatessen, with a gleaming white meat counter directly on the right as you entered. The second room, behind this, contained more grocery stock. This was a family enterprise, and while the Sciambra and Montalbano clan occupied the rest of the building—which grew with additional rooms as needed—everyone helped with the customers. And the customers came.

What drew them in was the Roma Sandwich.

"That sandwich was as big as a table," Frank Bruno, Sr., recalled. And you didn't just pick one up at the counter. Standing behind his meat counter, Mr. Montalbano looked through his heavy-rimmed glasses and contemplated his customer. If you wanted a Roma Sandwich, you had to design it yourself. "Whatever you wanted he'd put on it." While the customer chose each meat, salami, mortadella, prosciutto, then cheeses, provolone, mozzarella, then some homemade olive salad, the antipasto, Mr. Montalbano created his sandwiches to order. "Then he'd put it on the scale and you paid by the weight of what you ordered," Frank Bruno explained. As a young law student in the 1940s, Bruno was appreciative. "He didn't charge very much. That was the biggest bargain in the world."

Pat Ruffino recalled that Mr. Montalbano used "the best Italian bread." Besides the meat counter, "He had the little shelves in the back. He carried all sorts of delicacies from Italy. He had special olive oil, and delicious black olives."

Mr. Montalbano made a good sandwich, but he and his shop made an impact on everyone who entered. It was more than a grocery; it was a shrine.

At one point he called it "The Roma Room," but it was also known as the "Angel of Peace" sandwich shop. As his granddaughter Bernadette Patterson remembered, "There was an altar, with the angel over it. There was a huge statue of St. Joseph. In the back room there were candles and lights." When Bernadette grew up in the house, the telephone in the store could be reached at night only if you walked carefully around the statues and the altar until you saw a night-light in front of a small shrine to St. Joseph.

In addition, the back room walls were filled with holy pictures and a framed special blessing from the pope. Mr. Montalbano was always ready to give a customer a lucky bean—a fava bean, the bean that by intervention of St. Joseph had ended a great famine in Sicily. A lucky bean was sure to keep money in your purse.

And Mr. Montalbano demanded proper behavior from everyone who entered his shop. Joseph Miceli recalled, "He was a real perfectionist. Not that people generally cursed, but nobody could curse in there." And, as Frank Bruno remembered, "When you'd go in there, he wouldn't let anybody smoke. He'd say, 'You wouldn't smoke in church, would you?'"

Montalbano's devotion extended beyond creating his own little church. According to a postcard picturing him in his shop, he had held a parade for St. Anthony in thanksgiving for favors granted. And he regularly created an altar to St. Joseph on the saint's feast day, March 19.

According to Rosalie Serio Bilich, whose family had a St. Joseph altar in their Bourbon Street home, devotion to the saint was so intense that "you'd have thought St. Joseph was from Sicily—we never considered he might be Jewish." In the French Quarter there were altars in homes, to which the public was welcomed, and there might be an altar at St. Mary's gymnasium, and sometimes shops or restaurants might host one.

Frances Parkinson Keyes's 1941 novel *Crescent Carnival* has a section on the St. Joseph altars of the French Quarter, and one particular altar was a special attraction. In the book, it was located at "Montefiore's grocery."

"The room back of the shop . . . was papered entirely in religious chromos . . . and it was almost completely filled with an enormous table, only a narrow passageway being left around it. At one end of the table was erected a small shrine, enclosing a statue of St. Joseph and encircled with lighted candles and china figurines. But the rest of the table was laden with dishes heaped high with foodstuffs."

The St. Joseph altar described was at Montalbano's. Bernadette Patterson noted that "the table was marble. It was so heavy. It was in sections, and it did take up the whole room."

Mr. Montalbano did not end his devotions with parades and altars and his shrine. According to Frank Bruno, "He would ask you to make a little donation to his bread fund. Then every so often he would put his baker's cap on and go out with a basket of bread and give it to the poor people. He collected nickels and pennies all year for that."

Mr. Montalbano died in 1956. For a while, the family continued the shop. As Bernadette Patterson remembered, "After that, my mom and my uncle kept the place going. On Sundays, my grandmother used to make a big pot of meatballs, or sausages, and they would sell dinners in the back. She would make the antipasto in this huge bowl she had."

When the building left the family's hands, it went to Frank Bruno. "When I saw the place was available, I bought the building from the family." Mr. Montalbano's shrine had outlived him. "It was actually like he left it, the counters were in there, all of his holy pictures were on the walls."

Necessary renovations and rebuilding followed, and today no trace of the Angel of Peace sandwich shop remains, except in a memory of good tastes and good times and of a devoted sandwich maker who practiced his trade with his heart.

And there are still a lot of us who keep a lucky bean in a purse.

Hubig's Pies

IN NEW ORLEANS you would often see a rack or a box of these little desserts near the checkout counter—including in hardware stores. If there is a preferred dessert for New Orleans construction workers, it's the Hubig's Pie. Since the bakery burned in a disastrous fire in July of 2012, hungry Orleanians eagerly await their speedy return, certain that the familiar pie will remain the same.

There is a little smiling chef on the familiar Hubig's Pie wrapper—his hat reads "Savory Simon." As you might expect, there's a story behind it.

It started at the beginning of the twentieth century with Simon Hubig, a German-born baker who settled in Kentucky. Happily married, he tended his ovens and worked on his recipes. But when his wife died in 1912, Simon took his skills and began to travel.

By the beginning of World War I he was baking (probably in both senses of the word) in Fort Worth, Texas. Soldiers in training gave him an idea. Why not create something they could eat quickly (they were always in such a hurry) and that was filling (they worked so hard) and tasty (certainly they deserved a treat)?

Simon called his invention a "honeyfruit" pie. His fillings were sweet and good. He made round pies, small and big. He made a small, fried handheld pie—like the empanadas so familiar from Mexican cooking—and stuffed his with sweet fillings. There he had it—the perfect handheld treat!

With sweet success in Fort Worth, Simon decided to branch out. In a few years he had bakeries from Fort Worth to Cincinnati, with points in between. His bakeries had three hundred employees nationwide, and some local ownership. Simon was into franchising in a big way.

The New Orleans Hubig's bakery opened in 1922 and was man-

Hubig's Pies, as displayed at Castellon Pharmacy, 8232 Oak Street. Photo by Carolyn Kolb.

aged by two Texas brothers, R. Milton Jones and Windsor Jones. From their location at 2417 Dauphine Street they began producing pies, both baked and fried, for a hungry public. The New Orleans venture thrived, and the enterprising Jones brothers would become the sole owners.

When Simon Hubig died in 1935 his empire crumbled. All his bakeries closed, with the exception of New Orleans. There was something about those pies that fit right into local cooking—perhaps those spicy Creole flavors called for just such a sweet dessert.

In 1943 the Jones brothers were bought out by Henry Barrett, who loved his bakery so much that he kept coming to work almost until his death in 1991, at the age of ninety-one. In 1953 Barrett had added a partner, Otto Ramsey. Otto's son Toby joined the firm in 1970, and in 1972 Barrett—who had no children—invited his nephew Lamar Bowman to come over from Birmingham. Toby and Lamar are still active, but there is a new generation at the Simon Hubig Company these days: Toby's son Andrew "Drew" Ramsey and Courtney Bowman, Lamar's daughter.

Lamar, who has over forty years in the business now, worked as a bakery foreman for his first fifteen years.

Drew Ramsey, whose training is in business and management, took me through the bakery operation—both of us put on paper shower caps for the tour, pausing so he could introduce all the employees to me. On a huge round rotating machine there were screen racks to the ceiling filled with the familiar fried pies, fresh from their run through the fryer and the sugar waterfall and looking decidedly tasty. With their mechanized frying machine the Hubig Company can produce thirty thousand of these pies a day—and earned a place on a Food Network television show, *Top Five Extremes*.

Drew explained that he has one important rule: "Never have a stale pie on the market." As he explained it, each Hubig's Pie has a date number stamped on it. If the number is twenty-one, it means that pie cannot be sold past the twenty-first. "We give everything one week on the shelf, that's it," Drew said. So, pies marked twenty-one are delivered by Hubig's drivers on the fourteenth. Hubig's fries pies from Sunday through Thursday, and the deliveries go out (as early as 4 a.m.) from Tuesday through Friday.

"Our drivers will buy back the outdated pies from the stores for the same price the stores paid for them," Drew added.

Hubig's Pies are not only fresh; they have simple ingredients. "We buy locally whenever possible," Drew said. For Thanksgiving they will have seasonal sweet potato pies, made with Louisiana yams cooked on Dauphine Street. Fruit pies are made with the fruit they are labeled (not with a mixture of apple), the chocolate pies are made with cocoa, and the lemon pies have lemon oil. Flavors in fried pies include apple, lemon, banana, chocolate, coconut, and pineapple, with seasonal flavors of cherry, blueberry, raspberry, and sweet potato.

The handheld fried pies, "New Orleans Style Pies" as it says on their label, are the big sellers.

Where can you get a Hubig's Pie? Just about anywhere: grocery and convenience stores, marinas and Walmarts, schools (Brother Martin is one), factories (where they are sometimes in vending machines—"We ask for the lower slots so they don't have so far to fall," said Drew), on offshore oil rigs, in prisons, and from rolling lunch trucks.

The pies are also distributed outside New Orleans by LeJeune's Bakery of Jeanerette, as Hubig's distributes LeJeune's gingercakes to New Orleans sites. Another distributor goes to Mobile and the eastern shore of Mobile Bay. Apparently Hubig's Pies are well loved in Baton Rouge—according to the *Baton Rouge Advocate*, a Baton Rouge man faced a murder charge from a dispute over a Hubig's lemon meringue pie.

Hubig's Pies went with the fire truck given by Louisiana citizens to a Brooklyn fire station after 9/11. At least one Hubig's Pie was mailed to a soldier stationed in Iraq, according to Sheila Stroup's column in the *Times-Picayune*. There is even a poem, from the New Orleans Poetry Forum, by Cynthia St. Charles with the line "Hubig's pie blues for grown up Daddy's little girl."

In a quintessentially New Orleans way, Hubig's Pies are a big hit at my local hardware store, Freret Hardware at 5109 Freret Street. I once inquired about the pies. Delivered twice a week, the clerk said. Apple and lemon were the fastest sellers. I picked apple, fried. A roofer, waiting in line, commented, "You must be an old-time pie eater," and I allowed that I was. "I can remember when they cost a dime," he said. "Ooh, I'll be telling my age!"

Hubig's plant was damaged in Hurricane Katrina, but they recovered, as they will when they rebuild after the fire. Meanwhile, the website, Hubigs.com, is fully functioning. Until those pies are delivered again, check them out and visit their online store. A little support never hurts. (And it might get the pies back faster.)

Pralines

PECANS NOWADAYS most often appear in neat clear packages of shelled nutmeats. Orleanians also can encounter pecans underfoot, since the city is still dotted with the trees. Before Katrina, the wide neutral grounds by the University of New Orleans had huge pecan trees, their limbs sheltering a crowd of bent-over pickers when the annual crop hit the ground.

Pecan shells sometimes become garden mulch, but I can personally attest that a broken pecan shell is sharp enough to cut a gash in your scalp. Even when harmlessly encountered, pecans present difficulties: the meat is delectable, but getting it out is hard work. Christmas candy-making involved hours spent with a nutcracker. Luckily, Louisiana pecans are a cash crop, so they are both bountiful in season and available ready-to-eat.

The homemade pecan sweets I remember best were my grandmother's *graleéd* pecans—pecans tossed in a skillet with sugar until the sugar formed a crispy coating on the nuts. However, the most usual pecan candy, and the one commercially available, is the praline.

Pralines, described simply as "dainty and delightful confections" in *The Picayune's Creole Cook Book*, appear at the ends of buffet lines at receptions, are still occasionally sold from baskets by venders, pop up next to the cash register in shops, and are most often purchased as a souvenir or a little remembrance of New Orleans by tourists, or by locals for home use or as gifts.

Nuts coated with sugar were certainly known in the Middle Ages, and sugared almonds, sometimes called *dragées*, are a symbol of good luck and are still given out at christenings and weddings. The idea of a cooked sugar candy with nuts added is credited to the cook of the sixteenth-century French Duke of Plessis-Praslin, who gave his name to the treat. (The "s" in Praslin is silent. The word "praline" has its own

Aunt Sally's Praline Shop, 810 Decatur Street. Photo by Carolyn Kolb.

linguistic peculiarity—sometimes it gets pronounced "plarine." This switching of "l" and "r" is not unusual. Both are "liquid consonants" that can be easily slurred or elided in speech, hence the confusion.)

The original praline was made with almonds. No doubt when the French arrived in Louisiana and planted sugarcane (which they did by 1725), they substituted pecans, cooked them with the sugar they produced, and came up with the local version of pralines.

In *The Picayune's Creole Cook Book* there are recipes for a brown sugar praline, a white sugar praline with coconut, and a pink one made by coloring the coconut recipe.

Here is the praline recipe I like, adapted from a caramel icing recipe in the *Plantation Cookbook* of the Junior League of New Orleans:

> Toast two cups of pecans briefly on a tray in the oven. Combine one pound brown sugar, one cup whipping cream, and one stick butter in a saucepan and boil to softball candy stage. Take off the fire and add a teaspoon vanilla, stir till it

thickens, mix in the nuts, and spoon out in mounds on a buttered marble slab. Cool and cover each piece in plastic wrap, store in a covered tin.

While home cooks can produce pralines with ease in this day of the candy thermometer, specialty candy shops do a brisk business.

"People who buy candy are happy people!" asserts Mary Lou Quinn. She should know, as her days are spent making and selling goodies to her cheerful customers at Old Town Praline and Gift Shop, outside of Orleans Parish at 1506 Veterans Boulevard in Metairie.

Actually, she had been a branch bank manager with decades of financial experience when she took up the family candy business some years ago. Her grandmother, whose maiden name was Sieriex ("just say C-Rex") had originally worked for an owner of the Jacobs Candy Company who opened a French Quarter shop to sell pralines and gifts in the 1930s. "My uncle bought the business for my grandmother in 1964 and it's been in the family ever since," Mrs. Quinn explained.

Grandmother kept a keen eye on the candy making well into her nineties. "My grandmother lived nearby and my aunt and uncle and their family lived above the business," according to Mrs. Quinn. "We all grew up in the French Quarter. I went to St. Louis Cathedral School on Dauphine Street—actually four generations of my family went to school there." Mrs. Quinn's grandmother was French, but her mother's family "was from Sicily. They lived up above the tailor shop they owned on Chartres Street right by the Ursuline Convent.

"It was interesting growing up with all those different influences and foods," she remembers of her days in the Vieux Carré. The Old Town Praline and Gift Shop's last French Quarter location was at 627 Royal Street, where it had been since 1935. Ten years ago, after badly injuring her arm, Mrs. Quinn moved the shop to Metairie. "I love Metairie, but there's no place like the French Quarter. If you grew up there, it's in your blood!" Today, her daughter Patricia Weiss has joined her in the business.

Mrs. Quinn gets her pecans from Bergeron Pecans in New Roads, Louisiana, and she insists that her pralines are "different from everyone else's because we use no dairy products." Also, "we use a very old spooning technique, so when it's poured, it's smooth. It doesn't have a gritty taste." As she explains, she "grains" the pot. "We pull the sugar along the side of the pot." Thermometers help, but "you can tell by looking at the bubbles if you've done it long enough," she said.

In addition to pralines, Old Town offers heavenly hash (chocolate with marshmallow), chocolate-covered marshmallows, and "Clumpps" of sugared pecans mounded together. And there is a new treat: Katrina Debris, invented for the WYES-TV chocolate fundraiser. Mrs. Quinn describes it as "a crunchy hash: it's really good!" A new business venture includes weddings: "We not only do the candies, we do the second-line umbrellas, hankies, and wedding favors." And, there is a website now, oldtownpraline.com.

Will she keep it up? "You just can't let an eighty-year-old business go away, it has a heart!" Mrs. Quinn added.

Eva Louis Perry is a Louisiana native, but she first ventured into the food business in California. In 1987, she came back to New Orleans, and, as "Tee-Eva" (a shortened local form of "Auntie Eva"), used her grandmother's recipes to sweeten her entry into the local food market. Now Tee-Eva's own granddaughter, Keonna Thornton, presides over Tee-Eva's Shop at 5201 Magazine Street, dispensing regular and coconut pralines, pecan pies (regular and mini-sized) and even snowballs, besides other New Orleans food classics like jambalaya and red beans. According to Keonna, the schoolgirls from Xavier Prep School across the street are regular afternoon customers, and, besides deliveries to local shops and groceries, you can get your Tee-Eva specialties by ordering online at www.tee-evapralines.com.

Another family candy company has expanded from a single shop to a corporation with Internet presence and widespread distribution of their wares. Aunt Sally's is the trademark logo for a Creole praline as well as other candies and related products from the Bagur family–owned company. The Bagurs operated a little shop in the Vieux Carré as early as 1910, and began selling pralines in the 1930s, quickly moving into a French Market stall location—where Aunt Sally's can still be found.

The name Aunt Sally's was taken from a Vieux Carré street vendor whose pralines were remarkably good, according to the Bagur children. When their father, with the help of a Swiss confectioner, perfected a praline recipe, the two Bagur sons sold the wares themselves, sometimes from baskets at cemeteries on All Saints Day, when good Creoles visited their late relatives and met their friends and neighbors.

The company grew to several stores and a brisk mail order business, with their logo proudly displayed on delivery vans. Patricia McDonald Fowler, a family member, headed the company for over a decade, and fondly remembers Mardi Gras Day when the family gathered at their French Quarter shop on Royal Street.

Nowadays Aunt Sally's has a board of directors made up of family members, but a chief executive officer who is not a relation, Larry Statton. After Katrina, they were reopened in the French Market, the first confectionary store back in the French Quarter, on October 3, with a short labor team of six people.

Prior to Katrina, Aunt Sally's used 75,000 pounds of pecans and 180,000 pounds of sugar annually—that's certainly a sweet Louisiana product! The company is quickly cooking up new goals, and the French Market store manager, Becky Hebert, notes that Aunt Sally's pralines are "still made in copper pots, all hand cooked and hand poured and hand boxed."

Ms. Hebert added that Aunt Sally's offerings include the original "Creole praline" plus chocolate pralines. And there is now a new praline on the market: "Our creamy pralines are thicker and a little more fudgy, and they come in four flavors: original flavor, triple chocolate, café au lait, and bananas foster." Longtime cook Sam Hill can be watched as she stirs and ladles the creamy treats in Aunt Sally's French Market location at 810 Decatur Street, while the pungent aroma of hot sugar wafts over the sidewalk.

A melt-in-your-mouth, only-in-New-Orleans treat, the humble praline is ready to survive anything, even a Katrina.

Beulah Ledner and Doberge Cake

Doberge cakes are a New Orleans tradition and fantastic sweet dessert. There is something incredibly celebratory about having a birthday cake in so many, many layers. I am one of those who can never decide whether I like the chocolate, or the lemon, or the caramel doberge best. Personally, I like the little squares, rather like ornate petit fours, so you can have one of every kind at one seating. None of this would have been possible without a remarkable woman.

"Oh, Mimi made the most beautiful roses!" photographer Catherine Ledner said of her grandmother's skill with sugary icing. When Catherine was a teenager she worked in the Metairie bakery where her "Mimi," Beulah Ledner, created confections that delighted Orleanians for years. A granddaughter's fond memories are shared by the many who enjoyed the products of Beulah Ledner's ovens over nearly half a century.

Architect Albert Ledner explained that his mother, born Beulah Levy in St. Rose, Louisiana, had begun selling her baked goods out of their home kitchen in the university section when the family's financial situation demanded a creative solution in the Depression years. "Mrs. Charles Ledner's Superior Home Baking" was soon relocated to the basement of a raised house at 1200 Lowerline Street where Albert's grandparents made room in their home for the young family and Beulah's baking enterprise.

The recipes that Beulah had learned from her own mother had a strong German influence, and some were traditional Jewish sweets. In what would be her most memorable creation, a Hungarian specialty was deftly adapted to Louisiana palates.

The dobos torte—a dessert made up of many thin layers of cake with filling in between the layers and the whole cake then frosted and

Beulah Ledner's recipes are found in *"Let's Bake" with Beulah Ledner: A Legendary New Orleans Lady,* by her daughter Maxine Wolchansky, Atlanta: Let's Bake, 1987. Courtesy of the Nadine Vorhoff Library, Newcomb Center for Research on Women, Tulane University. Used with permission of Steve Wolchansky.

The Gambino Bakery purchased the Ledner doberge recipe and still makes the cakes, as shown on this billboard. Photo by Carolyn Kolb.

decorated—is still popular in Hungary, where it was supposedly created in the 1880s by confectioner Jozsef Dobos.

The first change Mrs. Ledner made was in the name—"dobos" doesn't sound very French, and knowing that Orleanians loved their French pastries, she cleverly settled on "doberge"—which sounds about the same.

Mrs. Ledner's version used, instead of the heavier butter cream, a lighter custard filling between the layers (she preferred nine separately baked very thin layers). The butter cream, however, would eventually cover the entire cake, and another icing would top that. Chocolate and lemon were the most popular flavors, but there was also a caramel version at one time.

In the early years on Lowerline Street, the family home housed not only the bakery but also a tearoom where lunch and dinner were served.

Albert Ledner and his sister Maxine took this family venture in stride: "To tell you the truth, as a youngster I really didn't think about it. I thought it was very nice." Albert recalled that the Newcomb College faculty and students frequented the tearoom, and the Ledner family dinner would take place each evening with guests at the other tables.

It was always a family venture. "My sister and I were expected to help out, not cooking or baking, but folding cake boxes and making deliveries," Albert said. Charles Ledner eventually became the full-time business manager, and other employees, including the fondly remembered African American baker, Bertha Jackson, made the enterprise grow.

Beulah Ledner created coffee cakes, layer cakes, birthday cakes, cookies, candies, tea sandwiches, and wedding cakes. Her kitchens could supply anything Orleanians needed for a party, and the business expanded. The bakery moved to 928 Canal Street, where it occupied an upper floor but had a display window at ground level. In later years the bakery moved to 2721 South Claiborne Avenue.

In 1946, after having struggled with rationing during World War II—a sore trial for a baker—Beulah Ledner's health forced her to close the business, and the complete "Mrs. Charles Ledner" bakery was sold to the Gambino family.

After two years of enforced idleness, Beulah Ledner was ready to get back to the mixing bowls. So as not to compete with her prior bakery, in 1948 she moved her business out of New Orleans, and used her own name, Beulah Ledner, in a new location at 2513 Metairie Road in Jefferson Parish. Her husband, Charles, died a few years later, but Beulah Ledner's bakery kept growing. She increased wholesale business, she became the official supplier of cakes to such demanding clients as the Boston Club, and at one point she even had frozen doberge cakes available in supermarkets throughout the area.

By the time of the frozen doberge venture, Beulah Ledner had a new marketing person, her daughter-in-law Judy Ferguson Ledner. And, of course, she baked the cake when Judy married Albert.

"We had the wedding at my home, so it wasn't a huge cake. But it was very pretty—three-tiered, the almond cake and white icing and butter cream, with roses on top," Judy remembered. Beulah, as "Mimi," was a fond grandmother, always ready to supply extra treats ("I really liked her plum kuchen," Judy added).

The Metairie Road location proved to be too small, and Albert was the architect and designer for a new bakery. The new location at 3501 Hessmer Avenue, also in Metairie, opened in 1970, and was her last location. (Maurice French Pastries occupies the building now.)

Besides tending to her business and her family, Beulah Ledner believed in giving back to her community. In 1977, her friend Chef Warren LeRuth invited her to join him, Chef Gofreddo Fraccaro, and Chef Chris Kerageorgiou in the newly formed Chefs' Charity for Children benefiting St. Michael's Special School. At the age of eighty-four, Beulah Ledner happily supplied apple kuchen for a dessert.

Beulah Ledner finally retired, at the age of eighty-seven, with her last workday being Mother's Day of 1981. The community did not forget her. Her friends, the chefs, even gave a special luncheon in her honor at Willow Wood Home when she was a resident there.

The best way to honor a genius in the kitchen is to share her recipes in a cookbook. *"Let's Bake" with Beulah Ledner: A Legendary New Orleans Lady* first came out in 1987 and is now out of print ("Google" that title on the Internet to look for a copy).

Maxine Ledner Wolchansky, her Atlanta-based daughter, in her introduction to the collection, wished this for readers: "May you receive as much joy from Mom's recipes and life history as I have . . ."

When work on the cookbook began, Albert Ledner had the task of cutting commercial-sized recipes down to family size. The all-important testing of the recipes required skilled help. Beulah Ledner worked with her daughter-in-law Judy and Judy's friends Janice Barton and Olivia Bamforth, and the four women would gather in the kitchen at Temple Sinai and bake.

Judy and Olivia had long been friends, and shared a love of the theater—and, in fact, had regularly performed short programs together for local audiences. Fortunately Olivia also loved to bake, and today continues to bake her own rum cakes, which she markets through Martin's Wine Cellar for the benefit of her church, Trinity Episcopal.

In what proved to be an ecumenical cooking spree (during which the Episcopalian helped produce a Seder dinner), the women carefully baked each cookbook recipe. Beulah Ledner supervised. "Mimi was still cooking. She told us what to do. Her memory was really very good," Olivia explained.

Beulah Ledner died at the age of ninety-four. Her legacy is a sweet one, perhaps best expressed in a tribute to her in her cookbook from a fellow cook, the late Warren LeRuth (the local chef who invented green goddess salad dressing and had a fabulous restaurant across the river).

"Dobos" and "dobas" and "doberge" can be spelled many different ways, but "if anybody asked me, I'd tell them it should be spelled L-E-D-N-E-R," said Warren LeRuth.

Nectar Ice Cream Sodas

YOU KNOW THAT SOUND you make when you suck on a straw and there is nothing left at the bottom of the glass? In my family we called that the "drugstore blues" (and you weren't supposed to make that rude noise, either). Well, when there is nothing left of your nectar ice cream soda, you have good reason to be blue. That is the quintessential fountain treat.

New Orleans has always been an ideal place to enjoy a soda, preferably with whipped cream. John Besh's new retro soda fountain at the World War II Museum is not only charming new converts to the ice cream soda craze, it's bringing nostalgic smiles to every Orleanian who ever sat at the Katz & Besthoff counter with a nectar ice cream soda.

There is a long soda tradition in New Orleans. The *Times-Picayune* in 1842 ran an announcement "To members of the Temperance Societies" heralding the opening of a "Refreshment Saloon" at the Planters' Hotel. Cost of every item on the menu was a "picayune"—six and a quarter cents. Ice cream, soda water, tea, coffee, chocolate, and orgeat were offered as refreshments. Orgeat syrup, a sweetened almond concoction, is comparable to the flavoring for nectar sodas. Although current commercial nectar syrup producer Susan Dunham gives credit to the I. L. Lyons Drug Company for producing nectar syrup locally, beginning around 1900, it is possible that the local fountain favorite is closing in on its second century of popularity.

By May of 1848, the *Picayune* noted that "soda fountains are fizzing away in all directions" and it continued over the years. Prices did increase, however. In 1935, Liggett's Rexall Drug Store on Canal Street advertised a nectar ice cream soda for ten cents. By 1947, the soda at K & B was twenty cents, including whipped cream. By May of 1955,

Nectar ice cream sodas were once a staple at the classic soda fountain at the Royal Pharmacy, 1101 Royal Street. Photo by Carolyn Kolb.

the price had gone up to forty-eight cents—but that included a bacon, lettuce, and tomato sandwich.

Dr. Stephen J. Derbes had his favorite drugstore: "Mayeaux's—it was right on the corner of Jefferson Avenue and Magazine Street." His favorite soda flavor? "Chocolate, and it came in that cone-shaped glass. It was ten cents." His visits to that soda fountain were "with the neighborhood gang. We'd go there and we would stay around and read the comic books."

Jack Stewart, whose favorite flavor was nectar, became a connoisseur of soda fountains around town. "At Arnaud's Drug Store, on Willow Street and Carrollton Avenue, they served sodas with big metal holders that the glass fit in, a big bell that tapered down.

"I went to Waterbury's on Canal Street at Camp Street. It was old-fashioned. At the Walgreens on Iberville and Royal streets, the lady used to put a little bit of crushed ice in to make it colder. The Woolworth's store on Canal and Rampart Street had sodas longer than the Woolworth's on Bourbon Street and Canal did," Stewart continued.

"I went to a lot of K & B's, both the old store and then the new store on St. Charles and Napoleon Avenue.

"The most spectacular was Walsdorf's Pharmacy, on Dryades Street at Peniston Street. It was run by George A. Walsdorf. The soda fountain was entirely white marble. It had a pressed tin ceiling, Belgian tile floors, metal soda fountain tables with either marble or white glass on the tops, soda fountain metal chairs. Mr. Walsdorf also made his own cough syrup called 'Why-cough,'" Stewart remembered.

Perhaps Stewart's fondest soda memory was also somewhat painful. Belou's Pharmacy on Marengo at South Liberty Street was a special favorite. "St. Cyr Belou would give you two squirts of syrup, when his associate Mr. Lorio only gave you one." Near this treasured dispensary of nectar sodas was an inviting overhanging tree. Stewart climbed up, but luck was not with him. After the fall he was bedridden while his broken bones healed.

Mr. Belou knew just what to do. "He made me this gigantic nectar soda, in one of those big, white, tubular cardboard containers. And that was right when they were closing the store," Stewart recalled.

Actually, you do not have to break a leg or even go out to a soda fountain to have a nectar soda. You can make your own nectar syrup, with this recipe from *Recipes and Reminiscences of New Orleans*, the Ursuline Academy Parents' Club cookbook:

> Cook three cups of sugar in one and a half cup of water, boil ten seconds. Cool and add one tablespoon vanilla extract, two tablespoons almond extract, and one-half teaspoon red

food coloring. Pour an inch of syrup in a glass, add a scoop of vanilla ice cream and club soda. Serve with a scoop of ice cream and whipped cream and a cherry on top.

Justin Winston admits he once lived for a summer on K & B nectar sodas and hot dogs. His best (and last) K & B soda memory was from a very odd location. "The building, where the Contemporary Arts Center is now, was the K & B warehouse. But, there was also a drugstore in it—in the middle of this enormous space. They had an operating soda fountain, too."

Winston had accompanied photographer Clarence John Laughlin to the soda fountain in question, but not just for the nectar sodas. "He wanted to see his pictures—there were four or five prints of his photographs. He had them made at the New Orleans Blueprint Company and they were enormous—maybe eight feet by ten feet. They were hanging in the warehouse."

Sodas in New Orleans can lead you to art—or to a quintessential New Orleans childhood memory.

Ann Maylie Bruce's parents, Anna May and Willie Maylie, were genial restaurant owners, and also enjoyed their cocktails at home.

Ann recalled that "we were living on Napoleon Avenue, I must have been about four. My aunt came over and she offered to take me to the K & B on Napoleon at Claiborne Avenue to the soda fountain."

As she described the rest of the adventure, "We sat on the little stools and the lady came up to me and said, 'Little girl, what kind of soda do you want.'"

"And I said, 'Scotch and soda, please.'"

"My aunt said, 'She means chocolate,' and I said, 'No, I don't.'"

They went right home.

Someone had just found the one item they never had on the fountain menu.

Food Bibliography

New Orleans is a place where the pleasures of the table are respected. The city even hosts the Southern Food and Beverage Museum (SouthernFood.org) in the Riverwalk shopping complex at the foot of Poydras Street. (The museum soon will be relocating to a new space on Oretha Castle Haley Boulevard.) And there is a large cookbook collection at the Nadine Vorhoff Library of the Newcomb Center for Research on Women on the Tulane University campus.

New Orleans Chefs' Cookbooks

Chefs publish their own collections of recipes—and these can provide wonderful and imaginative dishes. Here are some stellar names to stir up your interest: John Besh, Emeril Lagasse, Donald Link, Paul Prudhomme, and Susan Spicer.

Besh, John. 2009. *My New Orleans: The Cookbook: 200 of My Favorite Recipes & Stories from My Hometown*. Kansas City, Mo.: Andrews McMeel Universal.

Lagasse, Emeril. 2003. *From Emeril's Kitchens: Favorite Recipes from Emeril's Restaurants*. New York: W. Morrow/Harper Collins.

Link, Donald. 2009. *Real Cajun: Rustic Home Cooking from Donald Link's Louisiana*. New York: Crown Publishing Group.

Prudhomme, Paul. 1984. *Chef Paul Prudhomme's Louisiana Kitchen*. New York: W. Morrow/Harper Collins.

Spicer, Susan, and Paula Disbrowe. 2007. *Crescent City Cooking: Unforgettable Recipes from Susan Spicer's New Orleans*. New York: Knopf Doubleday Publishing Group.

New Orleans Home Kitchen Cookbooks

There may have been older New Orleans cookbooks, and there may be more famous ones, but *The Picayune's Creole Cook Book*, first published at the turn of the twentieth century, is my go-to book for classic New Orleans recipes and ingredients. The proportions and the instructions may be outdated, and the vegetables are cooked too long for our tastes, but this book has culinary secrets buried in every dish. Whatever edition you get, you will use this cookbook.

The Picayune's Creole Cook Book. 1938. 9th ed. New Orleans, La.: The Times-Picayune.

Hurricane Katrina ruined many a home recipe collection of clippings from the *Times-Picayune*. The paper's food editor, Judy Walker, joined with columnist, culinary instructor, and cookbook author Marcelle Bienvenu to bring out this collection of recipes from the newspaper's food section.

Bienvenu, Marcelle, and Judy Walker, eds. 2008. *Cooking up a Storm: Recipes Lost and Found from the Times-Picayune of New Orleans*. San Francisco: Chronicle Books.

New Orleans public utilities used to be under a corporation called New Orleans Public Service, Inc. NOPSI wanted every home to have lots of kitchen appliances to use those utilities, so they encouraged home cooking, and had home economists on staff who regularly published and distributed recipes. Entergy Corporation acquired the utilities and the recipes, and published this collection of old local favorites.

From Woodstoves to Microwaves: Cooking with Entergy. 1997. New Orleans, La.: Entergy Corporation.

Collections of home recipes are a popular way to form a cookbook, while at the same time giving a nod to the talent of home cooks. In New Orleans, and, in fact, in the state of Louisiana, these home recipes—whether they originated with the lady of the house or with the cook who came up with the recipe in the first place—give a good idea of the tastes of the past, and they also use simple, old-fashioned ingredients. You can travel the state through the taste of these dishes. There are various editions for each of them—any would be acceptable, but these are my favorites:

Jones, Elaine Douglass, Mrs. W. Elliott Laudeman, and Elaine Friedrichs Jones. 1975. *Gourmet's Guide to New Orleans: Creole Cookbook and Directory of New Orleans Restaurants*. Baton Rouge, La.: Claitor's Publishing Division.

River Road Recipes: By the Junior League of Baton Rouge, Inc. 1959. Baton Rouge, La.: The Junior League of Baton Rouge.

Talk about Good! Recipes Contributed by Members of the Lafayette Service League, Their Relatives and Friends. 1977. Lafayette, La: Lafayette Service League.

This New Orleans Junior League cookbook was the group's first. While the recipes are not credited to a single originator, every recipe was tested by members, and every recipe works. I do like the caramel icing for the brownies!

The Plantation Cookbook by the Junior League of New Orleans. 1972. New York, N.Y.: Doubleday and Co.

Howard Mitchum was a French Quarter character who was an amazing cook. This seafood cookbook has recipes, anecdotes, his artwork, and random information about New Orleans jazz, which he loved. The recipes work. I especially like his redfish courtboullion. Mitchum ran a restaurant in Provincetown, Massachusetts, for years. If you want to know more about his eccentricities, read his one-time employee Anthony Bourdain's 2001 memoir, *Kitchen Confidential: Adventures in the Culinary Underbelly* (London: Bloomsbury).

Mitchum, Howard. 1978. *Creole Gumbo and All That Jazz: A New Orleans Seafood Cookbook*. Reading, Mass.: Addison-Wesley Pub. Co.

Constance Snow is a gifted (and funny) food writer, and her work at the *Times-Picayune* was memorable. She has produced admirable cookbooks, and this is her take on foods along the Gulf Coast (which, of course, includes New Orleans and Louisiana). Plus, she's got my family's filé gumbo recipe in there!

Snow, Constance. 2003. *Gulf Coast Kitchens: Bright Flavors from Key West to the Yucatán*. New York: Crown Publishing Group.

Tom Fitzmorris parlayed a love of food and a knack for journalism into his current position as a one-man shop of restaurant critiques, his own website (nomenu.com) with restaurant ratings and feature stories on food—you can subscribe for more information or just be an occasional user—and a regular radio show with call-ins on food topics and interviews with chefs. Plus, he writes cookbooks and teamed up with New Orleans's Peggy Scott Laborde, documentary maker and local historian at WYES-TV, for a look at vanished local restaurants and their dishes.

Fitzmorris, Tom. 2010. *Tom Fitzmorris's New Orleans Food: More Than 250 of the City's Best Recipes to Cook at Home*. New York: Stewart, Tabori & Chang.

Laborde, Peggy, and Tom Fitzmorris. 2011. *Lost Restaurants of New Orleans*. Gretna, La.: Pelican Publishing Company, Incorporated.

Books about New Orleans Cooking

While these are not cookbooks, both of these books give a personal cast to Orleanians' love of food, and the intricate relationships that follow. Sara Roahen was a restaurant reviewer for *Gambit Weekly*, and both she and Randy Fertel are skilled and interesting writers. Randy's personal take on the success of his mother Ruth Fertel's steakhouse is an intriguing story, well told.

Roahen, Sara. 2008. *Gumbo Tales: Finding My Place at the New Orleans Table*. New York: W. W. Norton.

Fertel, Randy. 2011. *The Gorilla Man and the Empress of Steak: A New Orleans Family Memoir*. Jackson, Miss.: University Press of Mississippi.

PART TWO

Mardi Gras

Mardi Gras is such an intrinsic part of every Orleanian's inner calendar that, for those who are away from the city in the first quarter of the year, life seems unbalanced. Why isn't this coffee cake ring decorated in purple, green, and gold? How come no one is drinking out of garishly decorated plastic cups? How could they think "Mardi Gras Mambo" is a Latin dance number?

The rest of the world just doesn't seem to get it. Or, they get it wrong. Mardi Gras has a lot more to it than people pulling up their shirts to get beads thrown at them (although that sort of thing goes on, too). Mardi Gras itself changes and evolves. Plus, each year you might experience a different Mardi Gras yourself.

Mardi Gras actually is part of Carnival season—which runs from January 6, the Feast of the Epiphany or Twelfth Night that starts it off, through Mardi Gras, "Fat Tuesday," which ends at midnight when Lent begins. The archdiocese's own count shows that the metropolitan area is less than 40 percent Catholic today, but there is an underlying religious concept of feasting and partying before a period of fasting and repentance that Orleanians seem to naturally understand.

January 6 is also known as King's Day—that is, when the three kings arrived on the nativity scene. Orleanians celebrate this by eating king cake. King cakes, in the taste memories of myself and many other residents, should be not terribly sweet, but rather stale, round, flat, brioche-style cake circles with purple, green, and gold sprinkled areas of colored sugar on top and a plastic baby hidden inside. And they came from McKenzie's Bakery. You buy a king cake, bring it to work or send it to school or invite people over to share it, and the person who gets the baby has to bring the next king cake. This goes on until Mardi Gras. No matter that McKenzie's Bakery exists only in memory, the king cake endures: sweeter, fatter, softer, and available filled with various fruit fillings. And they now show up year round.

The most difficult king cake problem? Providing a king cake for a kindergarten class: you bring twenty babies so everyone gets one.

Mardi Gras has two main performance areas: the balls and the parades. Both have onlookers and participants. Participants include members of the sponsoring club, called a krewe, and their guests, either invited or paid or just present along the route.

Mardi Gras balls are, admittedly, an acquired taste. Granted, many krewes today, especially the super krewes like Endymion, Bacchus, and Orpheus, have big celebrity-laden parties with hot music and general dancing by all. If that's not enough, there are krewes of all sorts—women's krewes, gay krewes, krewes with miniature floats, krewes in all the communities around New Orleans and scattered through the state. There is even the krewe of Barkus for dogs (and some other pet krewes, too).

Balls held by the old-line krewes are a different matter. In the older krewes, women don long gowns, and in the more social of the krewes, white tie and all the full dress regalia (*coutume de rigueur* on the invitations) are worn by male guests and committee members (who do the actual calling out), and by krewe and officers of Rex. Other krewes' members wear costumes.

At this variety of Mardi Gras ball, krewe members are in costume, there is an orchestra, a grand march or procession of maskers, and the royalty of the evening: a king, queen, maids and their escorts. Invited guests, in formal attire, watch the proceedings. There will be *tableaux vivante*—posed scenes from a story or myth that is the ball theme—and then dancing. Masked krewe members will "call out" ladies in the audience (and someone from the committee does call out names in a special section by the dance floor) for a dance, and will present them with a krewe favor, a little trinket, perhaps in keeping with the ball's theme or the krewe's name. General dancing will follow, and afterwards the queen will entertain at a supper, sometimes with more dancing. The best late-night breakfast menu at a queen's supper should always include grits and grillades (gree-yades: tender cooked round steak in brown sauce or gravy).

Mardi Gras is basically about pleasure, for everyone who takes part. But it had its limits on participation. Back in 1992, city council member Dorothy Mae Taylor introduced an ordinance calling for

Carnival krewes to be nondiscriminatory in their memberships if they were going to parade on city streets. Some old-line krewes, Comus, Momus, and Proteus, ceased parading. Proteus has returned to the streets, and Momus evolved into Chaos. And, along the way, krewe membership quietly became more inclusive.

As far as parades go, what's not to like about putting on a mask and riding a float? Or strutting down the street in costume with your fellow club members? And what's so bad about having a huge audience cheering your every move and begging for your attention and your generosity?

And Mardi Gras balls? How can anyone complain about wearing an evening gown every so often? There is also something to be said for admiring someone in their royal finery (even if it's a male relative in a doublet and tights), and there are actually receptions at home for friends to view someone getting ready to reign. Best of all are those nice call-out favors the krewe members give their dancing partners.

At a parade, the masked krewe members ride on huge tractor-drawn floats and toss trinkets (beads, coins called doubloons, small toys—all of which are called "throws") to the crowds along the route, who scream, "Throw me something, mister!" In Zulu, which has become a very large parade and follows the standard route on Mardi Gras morning, decorated coconuts are the prized hand-out (too heavy to be thrown). The female krewe Muses hands out decorated shoes.

Every parade has a theme—in the larger and older ones the floats carefully reflect the topic. In some lesser parades, riding on rented floats, the theme may be limited to the name cards on the tractors. And, some parades are known for their satire: Krewe du Vieux in the French Quarter is often hilariously bawdy. Chaos and Krewe d'Etat (ruled over by the Dictator) like to skewer politicians.

Bands, groups of dancers, horsemen, torch bearers (flambeaux carriers), all join in the procession, and the king, mounted on his throne with his pages beside him, leads his entourage through the streets. Families line the routes (sometimes chaining ladders together so their offspring have a better chance at monopolizing the throws.) Groups gather around barbeque pits and picnic tables and watch parade after parade in a sort of dazed satiety.

When I was a reporter for the *Times-Picayune* I worked on Mardi

Gras (not that most people would call it work). One year I marched in the middle of the band behind the king's float in Zulu. That was when Zulu pretty much had no fixed route; it started at a funeral home on Jackson Avenue and meandered along until it got to Claiborne Avenue downtown. The band was a marching brass band and they let me, my husband, and some friends wander along in the back row with the big sousaphone. Music, dancing, beer, and then you get to write a story about it afterwards. A perfect day.

Another year I started out at six in the morning with the Lyons Carnival Club, a marching club that paraded from beer stop (bar or accommodating family) to beer stop and included on their route the Home for the Incurables (a hospital now mercifully renamed) where the brass band played "Little Liza Jane." Club members sported decorated canes, trimmed with homemade crepe paper flowers to bestow on pretty girls along the route. The walking krewes still begin their routes uptown early Mardi Gras morning, but the flowers may now be silk or plastic.

The parades and balls generally fall within the Carnival season, with the climax on Mardi Gras night, when Rex (the titular civic sovereign of the season) visits the ball of Comus (the krewe with the best social credentials). This "meeting of the courts" is televised so the general public can view the extravaganza, scrutinizing the dresses and jewelry and critiquing the courts. (This is great fun and raises couch potatoes to the level of *pommes de terre soufflé*.)

Orleanians can choose their level of participation, and, since much of the krewe part of Mardi Gras is private, their level of disclosure.

For my part, I always walk over toward Magazine Street to see the Krewe of Thoth parade on the Sunday before Mardi Gras. Thoth is the last of the neighborhood krewes uptown, and families still can sit on their front steps to watch. Trust me, it is a pleasure to be invited over for a parade party if you know someone who lives on the parade route—you eat, you drink, you run off to watch the action and catch throws—it's fun.

On Mardi Gras morning I still wander around with one of the walking clubs, and occasionally I will get to Audubon Park at seven for the "Rex Run"—free Rex tee shirts and king cake and orange juice, the current Rex, and the Queen of Carnival, who always wins the race (which is started by the firing of a small brass cannon). I usually catch Rex on Napoleon before it turns on to St. Charles. Other events I frequent as required by friends and family ties, but like most other Orleanians I am often surprised at what I can get into when I least expect it.

Mardi Gras is such a big topic that I have not managed to cover all aspects of it. New Orleans has a gay Mardi Gras that draws costumed participants from across the globe—and there are gay krewes and balls as well. The Mardi Gras Indians with their beautifully decorated suits and feathery headdresses are definitely part of the scene—I can remember when you could tell a downtown tribe from an uptown tribe by whether or not their headpieces had "mummy crowns." Today there are more women and children involved in the Indian tradition. The Baby Dolls and the Skeletons are other African American masking groups that are going strong. And the beautifully costumed Krewe of St. Anne that marches through the French Quarter on Carnival Day—that is certainly a creative highlight.

The topics in this section give only a sampling of the variety of Mardi Gras lore. Gallier Hall, the old city hall on Lafayette Square, still offers stands for guests of elected officials and the parading krewe and forms the focus of the city government's Mardi Gras entertaining. Flambeaux carriers light up the night parades and this old tradition seems to have a lively future ahead. And what Mardi Gras parade isn't a little more authentic with horses and mules involved?

The Krewe of Babylon still parades at night, making the most of their new Thursday night status. (I well remember Babylon parading in the French Quarter before the parades were banned on those narrow streets.) Sadly, the Krewe of Virgilians is only a flamboyant Mardi Gras memory.

The organized Mardi Gras parties of the Bourbon Street Bounders and their fellow groups have been succeeded by newer traditions of partygoers. The local shops and dressmakers still manage to dress the queens and courts and make Mardi Gras magic each year. The big bands still keep the beat going at Mardi Gras balls all season long. The Jerusalem Temple is no longer a Mardi Gras venue, but the Shriners with their clowns and funny cars still appear in occasional parades.

The 1969 movie *Easy Rider* beckoned young people to come to

New Orleans Mardi Gras for a potent brew of sex, drugs and rock and roll, and its effects are still with us, not only on the streets, but also in some long-lasting community service projects of Tulane students and others.

No problem. That's the good thing about Mardi Gras. Every year we make new memories just as good as the old ones.

Gallier Hall

FROM THE BEGINNINGS of the Rex parade, dignitaries and city officials have watched the floats pass in front of Gallier Hall, once our city hall, on St. Charles just across from Lafayette Square.

Back in the late 1950s, Mayor Delesseps S. Morrison tried to switch routes and dignitaries over to the new city hall on Perdido Street, but it didn't stick. Somehow if it wasn't on St. Charles it wasn't right—for whatever reason, the mayor went back to Gallier Hall.

I myself once spent Mardi Gras Day in the Gallier Hall stands, sometime in the Morrison era. Sad to say, all I remember is that I was NOT TO SNATCH BEADS, especially if any adult in striking distance may have eyed them first. I know I must have worn my cowboy costume, but I can't recall seeing any celebrities, although they were rumored to be around.

One Orleanian was asked to go with Otto Preminger, famed Hollywood producer, to Gallier Hall for a night parade while Chep was mayor. Isabel Monteleone was acting as hostess, and all was very pleasant, until Mr. Preminger saw his first flambeaux carriers. He was appalled. "Why are they throwing money at them?" he demanded. No explanation sufficed. The movie he was supposedly scouting locations for was never made, at least not in New Orleans.

In the era of Mayor Vic Schiro the grown-ups were definitely enjoying the night parades. Register of Conveyances Gasper Schiro (no relation to Vic) notes that "it's the best place to watch a night parade, the floats are so beautiful." Gasper and his wife, Mel, credit Mayor Schiro and his wife, Sunny, with being genial hosts. "They really put on the parties, they served champagne. There were jazz bands. They believed in doing everything very elegantly," Gasper added.

In the era of Mayor Moon Landrieu all the arrangements for Gal-

Gallier Hall at Mardi Gras, circa 1910. Photo courtesy of the Louisiana Division/City Archives, New Orleans Public Library.

lier Hall and the stands were in the capable hands of Margaret Mary Falcon (now Mrs. Salvadore Mulé). After her city hall days, she celebrated Carnival Day by fixing red beans and rice for her extended family and catching Rex on Napoleon Avenue, but when Moon was mayor she was always at Gallier Hall.

"We had one section for the mayor and the other for the councilmen," Margaret Mary remembers. For the other stands, including those along Lee Circle, seats were marked, tickets were sold and ushers were hired. "There were thousands of tickets and I did it all by hand. I was doing tickets in the day, taking orders, and at night I would go over to Gallier Hall, and when it was over I would help pick up and then go home and go back to work the next day."

Margaret Mary remembers that a block of tickets always went to the trailer campers who gathered at City Park. Special arrangements were made for public service buses to pick up youngsters at children's homes for seating on the Lafayette Square side stands. "We gave money for one little girl from an orphanage to have a complete new outfit for Mardi Gras each year," she added.

There were official city doubloons that were handed to monarchs on their floats, along with a glass of champagne. Each parading krewe received Gallier Hall passes for their courts, and their guests were served drinks and hors d'oeuvres. The maids and queen wore their ball dresses to view the parade. "The Endymion court came in a moving van—their costumes were so big. That was before their maids started riding on floats," Margaret Mary explained.

"It was so hectic, just a whirlwind," she recalls. Celebrities blurred into the crowd. "But I do remember Billy Carter [President Jimmy Carter's brother]. He just wanted to be in the streets, but he kept coming back to the stands."

The popularity of watching parades from Gallier Hall continued through Mayor Dutch Morial's years (although one of those years saw no parades because of the police strike).

Under Dutch, Flo Schornstein remembers, "You had to go so early, and it was hard to park.

"Certain parade nights were more sought after than others for tickets," she added. The job of ticket distribution fell to Harriet Burnett on Morial's staff. "It was a real job," Flo explained. Ticket sales began to be looked on as a revenue source. Tightening budgets also brought other changes. The free buffets disappeared, as did the open bar.

During Mayor Sidney Barthelemy's administration, his wife, Mickey, made the mayor's Thursday night dress-up party a signature event—and when Momus didn't parade they still gave the party and had Mardi Gras Indian groups come in costume and stage a mock battle.

According to Mickey Barthelemy, "I thought it should be elegant, and that black tie attire should be strictly adhered to—I said I'm going to insist that people dress formally." In addition, "I just felt that it would be really fun if everybody wore a mask."

The idea caught on—masks were worn and tickets were so eagerly sought that some people even tried counterfeiting them. And Mickey sought out galleries and museums for Mardi Gras–themed decorations. "The Historic New Orleans Collection lent us some of the old Mardi Gras float designs, and mask makers sent us masks. It was beautiful," she said.

Those dress requirements were strictly upheld. "One of the doormen told me that a white limousine pulled up to Gallier Hall, and a couple got out, and presented their invitations. The lady was wearing a short dress and they were told that wasn't allowed. Her escort said, 'Don't worry, we'll just go get you a long one,' and he went and bought her a long dress and they came back to the party," Mickey related. Giving that annual party "was a lot of work, but I really did enjoy every minute of it," Mickey said.

Stacy Simms, who began at city hall in Mayor Marc Morial's administration, served as Mayor Ray Nagin's Director of Community Affairs and Special Events, and was "at Gallier Hall every day, for every parade that passed till the last vehicle had gone by."

Handling Mardi Gras duties for the mayor's office now is Mary Beth Romig, Director of Public Relations and Special Projects. Current New Orleans Mayor Mitch Landrieu watched many a parade at Gallier Hall when his father, Moon Landrieu, was mayor. Mitch is such a parade stalwart that, during a downpour, he was there to help the queen down from her float in the Iris parade.

Gallier Hall tickets today are distributed to the parading krewe (one hundred tickets), city council members (thirty passes to Gallier Hall and fifteen stand tickets per night), and the mayor's office has some, too. Food, plus beer and wine, is available for purchase. Krewes designate a narrator to read a script with the float descriptions for their parades—the mayor will often do this, or Mary Beth Romig might pitch in. The mayor will toast the king or queen, or grand marshall, and any other krewe royalty on the reviewing stand will join in the toast.

Ticket sales for all the stands now bring in substantial revenue. Travel agents buy up blocks, but special requests also come in, sometimes from as far away as China.

And when those round-the-world visitors get to Gallier Hall, they still get the best seats at Mardi Gras.

Light Up the Night: Flambeaux Carriers

BACK IN NEW ORLEANS in the immediate post-Katrina era, there were large areas of the city that had no lights at night. When we would drive through those neighborhoods, especially in the older parts of town near the river, the city had a special, spooky charm. With the old houses surrounding me in darkness, I could get a sense of what night in the city had felt like in the past century.

Sometimes at Mardi Gras, you get that same feeling of being in the past. Standing in the dark, maybe shivering in the cold, you wait in anticipation as you faintly hear the beat of the drums in the first marching band, and finally, out of the darkness, the fiery glow of the flambeaux pierces the gloom. A night parade is pure old-time Mardi Gras magic, and it's largely due to the flambeaux and their intrepid carriers.

Want a Mardi Gras you'll really remember? Want to be in a parade?

Consider this: you could get paid thirty dollars or so, plus tips, and prance along in front of a guaranteed audience ready to applaud your every movement—you, too, could carry a flambeau.

Flambeau carriers bear a heavy burden these days. Historically they have predominantly been African Americans, and their dancing antics carry an unwelcome message to some modern parade-goers. The Backstreet Museum, a shrine in Tremé with artifacts of Mardi Gras Indians and other masking traditions, does not celebrate flambeau carriers. Some see the flambeau carriers as symbols of society's inequities.

Flambeaux are still part of a long line of traditional Mardi Gras practices. In typical New Orleans fashion, something that was a necessity was changed and transmuted into a peculiarly local art form.

Flambeaux carriers, Mardi Gras 2012. Photo by Carolyn Kolb.

Flambeaux today come in different varieties—there is the old-fashioned tank and burners style (in variations on two and four burner options), the flare on a stick, the propane tank style, and even a toilet-paper-roll-in-a-tin-can-on-a-stick style favored by Slidell parade marchers.

Torches to light nighttime processions were a necessity back in the nineteenth century when there was little street lighting, but New Orleans flambeaux—using the French name for torch makes for a nice local touch—have persisted through the years. If you would like to see what the earlier flambeaux looked like, there is an example in the Louisiana State Museum. Or, just keep your eyes open when you see a night parade approaching: the older versions still can be found.

While early Orleanians might have regularly paraded through the nighttime streets in celebration, the first of what we know as organized Mardi Gras parades was the Comus pageant of 1857, which was lit by torches, most likely made with shredded rope soaked in pitch. The next year, Comus actually had what was described as a spotlight—possibly some piece of stage lighting equipment. New Orleans had gaslights in some form from the 1820s, but wider usage required piping and gas mains and this method was just not suitable for portable light fixtures.

The breakthrough in flambeaux manufacture came with an 1872 invention for a vapor-burning streetlight with a daisy-shaped burner. The wind-proof device held liquid fuel in a container, had a heater for the fuel and a burner for the resulting vapor, which then gave off light. Add a reflector and put the device aloft on a stick, and presto: a flambeau.

Just as the old Mardi Gras floats began with humble cotton wagons, so the flambeaux carriers began using pieces of cargo slings with leather reinforcing to fashion a pole holder to wear, with a stick to twist the belt tighter. That device, plus a head scarf covering and a loose smock to protect clothing make up the carrier's working outfit.

Is it dangerous work? Well, some decades back when gasoline was the fuel in use, it was much more hazardous than it is today. In the past, the better fuel was kerosene, which is relatively safe, but difficult to find. Today, the old-fashioned flambeaux use paint thinner or mineral spirits. What burns is the vapor. While gasoline vapor will ignite from a spark even if the temperature is far below zero, vapor from mineral spirits only ignites at a temperature of 104 degrees, high enough to require a flame to set it off.

Did the flambeau carriers always dance? Actually, parade planners didn't intend for them to. If you consider that the old-line night parade floats (Proteus is the only one still parading, but Babylon follows the old design) always have strips of metallic foil placed strategically in the design, you can see that the reflection of the light makes the parade more magical. Supposedly the ideal parade would have flambeaux on each side of a float, with their metal reflecting sheets facing toward the float, all the better to illuminate it for the crowd.

Another special lighting effect was the fusee, the flare on a stick that used to be carried in front of floats to provide a cloud of smoke. Sad to say, the Environmental Protection Agency changed the rules and those smoke sticks no longer exist. Just like the mist machines at rock concerts, the smoke magnified the effects of the flambeaux lighting, adding to the magic.

Flambeaux today, the vapor burning variety, are usually made with some type of stove burner. Manufacture is problematic: there must be a windshield, there must be a reflective sheet, and the entire device must be sturdy and practically indestructible. Several flambeaux were badly damaged in Katrina, and only some have been repaired. Proteus has its own old-time flambeaux; the rest in use come from various sources, old and new, and krewes rent or borrow them from each other. Endymion's propane-tank flambeaux are actually gas burners, and are sometimes referred to as "ghost busters" since they resemble devices used in that film.

Among the krewes that have used flambeaux in some form are Babylon, Bacchus, Chaos, Endymion, Hermes, Krewe d'Etat, Orpheus, Proteus, and Sparta. Will there be flambeaux at all those parades—or more—every year? It depends.

"Everybody likes flambeaux. The technology is easy. There are multiple sets of flambeaux. Yes, the prices are high. It's a lot of work, it's a labor of love. The problem is the missing ingredients. Everything is there but the carriers," noted one krewe member.

Prior to Katrina, flambeau carriers regularly appeared. Except for a strike in 1946 (wages went up the next year), the carriers showed up before a parade, and with police help, enough were chosen to fill all the spots. In fact, the Lazard family was recognized as organizers for the flambeau carriers and regularly filled the ranks with relatives and friends.

Katrina changed things. Not only did the old group of carriers not appear, but the new parade schedules with multiple parades in one night increased the number of carriers needed per evening.

College fraternity members, Hispanic construction workers, former carriers ready to give it another try—the krewes are crossing their fingers that enough eager workers show up three or so hours before parade time on Napoleon Avenue near Camp Street.

What's it like to carry a flambeau? John Carter says he's too old now, but he well remembers Mardi Gras past. "I carried a flambeau the last year we went through the French Quarter!" he said. "It's not hard if you know what you're doing." The most difficult part is at the beginning of the parade, because "it's heavy with a gallon of fuel still in there—and I liked the four burner better than the two burner, it burned off faster." As the fuel burns down, the flambeau is easier to carry and to dance with. "You want to get in the front of the parade, that way there's more money at the beginning. They'll even tuck the money in your belt," he remembered fondly.

One hopes that Mardi Gras will continue to be as Nancy Lemann described in her 1985 novel, *Lives of the Saints*, and a night parade will be "inexpressibly gaudy and beautiful as it passes along, bidding farewell to the flesh. There are always drumbeats haunting the parade, and flambeaux and harlequins in satin and silk."

Hot to Trot: Mardi Gras Horses

ANOTHER OLD-FASHIONED PART of Mardi Gras that is still with us is the use of four-footed animals. From mounted parade riders to mules pulling floats, Mardi Gras is still running on horsepower.

Several decades ago, a group of Mardi Gras krewe members gathered one night near some stables. Accompanied by flambeaux carriers and a few musicians, they proceeded to bang on kettles and yell while a group of waiting horses stood somberly watching with their grooms. "We just wanted to be sure they were parade ready," one krewe member remembered. "It was the first time we were renting from that stable."

Each year the lieutenants or officers of various parading Mardi Gras krewes will mount up to parade, masked, through the daytime and nighttime streets of New Orleans (and outside-the-city parade routes). And there are women riders. Caye Mitchell rides as "Warrior Joan" in the Joan of Arc parade, and also rides in Muses, Druids, and Thoth. Obviously they all want safe, steady mounts.

"Horses are great sports. They will do anything you ask," commented one veteran Mardi Gras masked rider, who owns a horse but does not bring it to parades. He admitted that the one spot on the uptown parade route he always has the assigned groom hold the lead rope (rather than guiding the horse himself) is underneath the expressway at Lee Circle. "That noise overhead can really spook a horse." And, in another nod to safety in the old-line krewes, "If you ride, you are discouraged from carrying throws."

The Hermes parade has at least one rider who is astride his own horse, and there have been others with their own mounts through the years, but the krewes rent horses for the majority of riders. A major supplier is Barbe Smith's Cascade Stables in Audubon Park.

Parade rider with throws, Mardi Gras 2012. Photo by Carolyn Kolb.

"We buy a lot of horses and bring them in and get them healthy. After Mardi Gras we sell some of them to really good homes, and we keep some to be our school horses," Ms. Smith explained. The Rex Parade alone uses thirty-five horses, and some nights Cascade supplies horses (each with a groom) to more than one parade.

"The captain will ride a white horse, General deGaulle," Smith said. For safety, "We use shoes with borium (tungsten carbide) on the bottom, and that keeps them from slipping, even if it's raining."

Another stable supplies the seven horses used by the Krewe of Sparta, and the horses ridden by the captain and his boy "shadow" are both white. Besides the krewe members who ride, parades will often have groups of riders, "posses" or riding clubs, who are part of the procession. And, the huge Budweiser Clydesdales will be represented in several parades, with eight horses pulling the traditional beer wagon.

The krewes of Sparta, Zeus, and Babylon also make use of mules in their parades.

In Sparta, "The king's float and our signature float are pulled by mules," the captain explained. Mid-City Carriages provides those mules.

Louis Charbonnet of Charbonnet's Mid-City Carriages explained that their thirty-five mules and fifteen horses are housed in stables right off North Claiborne Avenue near the Municipal Auditorium. The carriage company provides a driver for each vehicle the mules pull and also sends out grooms for the animals. "If we can, we send a vehicle along with them, a pooper-scooper, but sometimes they don't want our truck right behind a float."

Traditionally, New Orleans mules that pulled garbage trucks went to work pulling floats during Mardi Gras. By the 1950s, garbage trucks were motorized. Now, mules are only used sparingly, but Charbonnet still believes in mule power. "They are physically fit, and they work every day. Working is better than standing around the stable, so they enjoy working."

"If mules are being mistreated, if the harness is on wrong, they will let you know," he said. "And when they are ready to go home, they will tell you. You better head to the barn!" Charbonnet's mules regularly pull tourist carriages, and they will pull carriages in a French Quarter parade on Bacchus Sunday. When pulling floats in a parade, they will be wearing a white cloth covering.

While masked parade riders are ceremonial these days, the New Orleans Police Department maintains a mounted division year round. An officer on horseback can see above the crowd, get places more quickly than on foot, and all that additional height and bulk can be intimidating to wrongdoers. Plus, policemen on horseback are always crowd pleasers and that makes for good public relations.

It takes a special horse to be able to handle the rigors of crowd control, especially New Orleans crowds at Mardi Gras. Surprisingly, many dependable, experienced mounts are found behind the gates of Angola State Prison, where Stemmans, Inc., Horse Sales holds an annual October horse auction. As Charlotte Stemmans-Clavier explained, Angola horses are good buys because, at the prison, "they are still using horses in agriculture. Horses are pulling the plows and the cultivators. They still ride horses for work."

Horses are also bred at Angola. Percherons are large, heavily muscled horses, and the offspring of a Percheron and a thoroughbred horse is especially prized for police work. All government agencies, like the police department, buy directly from the prison. (You can get more information online at http://www.angolaprisonhorsesale.com.)

New Orleans Police Commander Jeff Walls will be spending Mardi Gras riding Dakota, a female Percheron-cross, a large horse well suited to parade season. The police horses will be working overtime during Mardi Gras, too, but they will get an extra holiday after the season.

Some police officers are full-time riders, and some ride on a part-time basis, but all get regular training. "Before any special events, we go out and do things with the horses. They all have their own personalities. Some are scared of flags, different moving things, noise, so we try to desensitize them," Walls said. The horses have a rubber-type shoe, and some of them are fitted with earplugs.

Mounted policemen have gone through crowd control training, too, and they are ready for any Mardi Gras shenanigans. But don't even think about hurting their horses.

As Commander Walls cautions: "They hit a horse, they go to jail."

So, when you hear hoofbeats at Mardi Gras, look and smile . . . but don't touch.

Babylon

EVERY ONE OF US has a favorite Mardi Gras memory—mine involves the year we wore monk's robes and had "church keys" around our necks—and, while that was memorable, it wasn't something to build a future career on.

But then, I'm not Henri Schindler, who could say of "the first night parade I ever saw" that "it changed my life!"

That's a strong statement from Mardi Gras guru Schindler, but he's happy to pay that tribute to a longtime Carnival club, the Knights of Babylon.

As Schindler explained, "There were no parades during World War II, and 1946 was my first Mardi Gras. I had turned five the day after Christmas. That Wednesday night I saw my first night parade, Babylon, and it's been on my mind ever since." Schindler watched the parade on Canal Street, between St. Charles Avenue and Camp Street.

"For me, what made it unique was that it was the one that kicked off the Carnival season—for many people the real season still begins with Babylon."

Schindler's deft artistic hands are now fashioning the look of the Babylon parade, through Kern Studios. Although historically it was a Wednesday parade, when the Krewe of Momus left the streets some years back, Babylon changed its schedule to parade on Thursday evening. The organization celebrates its seventy-fifth birthday in 2014.

Newspaper columnist Charles "Pie" Dufour once described Babylon as "one of the oldest of the 'newer' Carnival organizations." According to Babylon's captain, krewe tradition holds that the krewe began after a member of the Krewe of Hermes had a falling out with a relative who was the Hermes captain, and subsequently started a new krewe.

Babylon king's float pulled by mules, Mardi Gras 2012. Photo by Carolyn Kolb.

According to the Krewe's website, it was founded "on June 24, 1939, by a group of New Orleans professionals who wanted to stage a first-class Parade for the public and a first-class Tableau Ball for their ladies."

The parent organization is still known as the Jesters Club (besides a club pin, on special occasions members may wear a "Jester" tie, now available to them in both blue and raspberry colors). The shield of the club sports a Jester, holding masks of tragedy and comedy.

The krewe is properly called the Knights of Babylon, and the king is King Sargon of Akkad, commemorating the long-ago builder of the famed city of Babylon (once located in what is now the country of Iraq).

Babylon has some long family traditions: a founding member's daughter who once reigned as queen has had two daughters reign and her husband is a member. Pages regularly have a grandfather who is a member. One long-serving captain of Babylon was the late Dr. Charles Mary, a dentist.

Babylon is a strong upholder of Mardi Gras traditions. The identity of King Sargon is not made public. The parade is followed by a ball that night, with tableaux, and maskers' dances with call-outs to dances for invited ladies (who receive favors from their dance partners), and there is a supper dance (known in other krewes as the "queen's supper") afterwards.

Babylon owns its own floats which are stored in the krewe's own den. Of the floats, Schindler noted that while the undercarriages may not date to the 1800s, "They have the size and the feel of the old floats. They're not double-deckers, they are just a nice old size."

The king's float is actually one of the few remaining parade floats made entirely of papier-mâché. "It's a spectacular rolling antique," according to Schindler. Happily for Babylon members, their den stands on high ground and the floats suffered no damage in Hurricane Katrina.

Another special Babylon float is a streetcar, a copy of a mule-drawn "bobtail" car, the type used on New Orleans streetcar tracks from 1860 until 1890, and the era when electricity came into use. Babylon's streetcar float has a scene of the old Southern Railway station painted on its side. Schindler, who noted that the little painting was "very lovely, delicately painted," added, "I don't know for a fact who did it, but I know that Deutschmann Brothers was building the parade at that time, and it's very likely that one of them did the painting."

Schindler has been involved with Babylon for some years, and is pleased that he has worked to have some of the krewe's signature floats based on items from the history of Babylon, with the Hanging Gardens and the Gate of Ishtar among the topics used as inspiration. The 2012 parade theme, inspired by that year's king's affinity for all things English, was the Diamond Jubilee of Queen Elizabeth II. Schindler was especially proud of the float honoring Queen Elizabeth I, in all her flamboyant glory.

Babylon's captain promised that flambeaux will accompany the floats in each year's parade as they have in the past. One of the magical things about floats in night parades is that a glistening effect is achieved with metallic decoration. Schindler explained, "It's the final touch, but it's really essential.

"Silver and gold leaf are the last things that go on the floats," applied in small strips so that they glitter in the torchlight. "It's amazing that something so delicate is so resilient. The little end piece that isn't glued down flutters," he said.

Schindler described Babylon's parade as typical of old style, especially in the size of the floats and the number of floats. Babylon is "not too long," according to Schindler; "it leaves you wanting more."

In spite of its respect for Mardi Gras traditions, Babylon has been innovative, adding electricity to floats, and once having the king's float operated by a driver and carriage completely enclosed, in the manner of floats in California's Rose Bowl Parade—this was not continued for practical safety reasons, according to the captain.

One innovation by Babylon that has remained is the use of mules. Once mules pulled all parade floats, and in 1968, in homage to that idea, Babylon began using them for the king's float (which continues to this day) and for the streetcar float.

The 1968 parade went through the French Quarter, and rumor had it that the slow pace of the parade was inadvertently caused by the bell on the streetcar float. One of the mules, Baby, had supposedly left a day job pulling the Roman Candy Wagon, and was stopping every time the bell rang, in anticipation of a sale.

Babylon's captain once related that the streetcar bell has somehow been misplaced because of an occurrence some years back. The usual streetcar riders are the krewe's officers. One year pages were permitted to ride as well, and an overly enthusiastic page's bell ringing prompted an officer to remove the noisemaker. It has not returned.

Besides the officers in the streetcar float, the captain will be in a carriage, pulled by a white horse. Krewe members on horseback, the Horsemen, will lead the procession. The Knights of Babylon will be following the traditional parade route along St. Charles Avenue uptown, and they will proceed to Canal Street, where their ball will be held at the Sheraton Hotel.

Babylon balls were always held at the Municipal Auditorium. While Harrah's occupied that space, Babylon moved to the Theater of Performing Arts next door. Since Hurricane Katrina, Babylon has been at the Sheraton Hotel.

At the ball, King Sargon will use either the gold or silver crown and scepter set belonging to the krewe. The queen's crown and scepter are given to her as mementos. Royalty and the court of the past year will be honored, as will the dukes of the organization, and the maids, in matching white gowns, will be presented. According to Babylon custom, their bouquets will include orchids. Besides young boys as pages, young girls will be presented as ladies-in-waiting.

After the ball and supper dance, "We end our evening about four or five o'clock in the morning," the captain of the Knights of Babylon admitted.

Then he and Henri Schindler will get ready for the krewe's next year.

Virgilians: The First Super Krewe

THE VIRGILIANS are the stuff of Mardi Gras memories—the krewe dissolved some years ago, but it is still fondly recalled. A Virgilians ball invitation was something to be prized—and you had to be a truly hard-core ball aficionado to sit through one of their lengthy extravaganzas. I admit, I never attended Virgilians. My grandmother always said that people who loved opera would be the ones to appreciate that krewe—but then she never attended a Virgilians ball, either. I take it on trust that they were fabulous.

"People used to arrive at the Municipal Auditorium before noon and wait at the front door so they could get the best seats," Charles Cabibi, Jr., recalled. The Krewe of Virgilians, with his father, the late Charles Cabibi, Sr., as captain, presented its last ball in 1964. From its first Mardi Gras celebration in 1939, this predominantly Italian American organization was known for its elaborate extravaganzas.

Even the Virgilians' ball invitation was out of the ordinary. Virgilians invited guests to a "Costume and Scenic Spectacular," a "Spectacular Ball Production," or a "Spectacular Grand Ball Production." This was no ordinary tableaux-and-call-outs evening.

Virgilians' name came from the Roman poet Virgil. At a time when old-line Carnival organizations did not include Italian Americans in their membership, Virgilians offered a way for its members to present their daughters to society and have them reign as Carnival royalty.

According to a 1978 *Times-Picayune* article, Dr. Emile A. Bertucci spearheaded the founding of the krewe and did the research and wrote its productions for the first years of its existence—Cabibi, Sr., continued after Bertucci. The Virgilians' first ball in 1939 honored their heritage by commemorating Dante's *Inferno*—a classic Italian poetic work.

Appropriately, that first Virgilians program began with a poem, the lines of which each began with a letter spelling out the night's theme: DANTE'S INFERNO. The first verse read:

Down within the depths of Hell
And where arch sinners lustly dwell,
Nothing can partly relieve their pain,
Together do they cry in vain
Endless tortures are their lot
Sorrow, misery their souls to rot.

Sounds a little somber for a Carnival ball? Well, not exactly. Queen that year was Marguerite Piazza Luft (who went on to fame as opera singer Marguerite Piazza). She portrayed Francesca da Rimini, "Flame of Hades," and her sequined ball gown is displayed today in the American Italian Museum at 537 South Peters Street.

The Virgilians' annual themes were always expanded into grand productions with numerous scene changes, slide shows, ballets, and, always, music. Russ Papalia and his orchestra played for the early years, but by 1953 René Louapre was providing the music.

A complete list of the Virgilian ball themes includes (1939) Dante's Inferno, (1940) Ben Hur, (1941) Destruction of Atlantis, (1942–1945) cancelled for World War II, (1946) Dawn of Creation, (1947) The Great Deluge, (1948) Milton's Paradise Lost, (1949) Rossini's William Tell, (1950) Glorification of Life, (1951) Inner Sanctum of the Mental Realm, (1952) Metamorphoses of the Gods of Ancient Greece and Rome, (1953) World's Great Spectacles in the March of Time, (1954) Creative Imaginations of Great Men, (1955) Six Thousand Years of Sacred Events, (1956) Dante's Il Paradiso, (1957) Phaeton's Flight in the Sun God's Chariot, (1958) Myths and Legends of Mythology, (1959) Virgil's Aeneid, (1960) The Ten Commandments, (1961) A Pageant of Beauty and Splendor of Ancient Japan, (1962) The Theatre—An Extravaganza on Entertainment, (1963) The Birth and History of Opera, and (1964) Highlights of Enchantment.

Grandeur was the watchword. Virgilians had a silver curtain made for the auditorium. White canvas always covered the dance floor. Whatever the theme required, Virgilians supplied. There was an actual chariot, with horses, for Ben Hur. Moses parted the Red Sea on

The last maid of Virgilians, Romelia Boyer Schiro. Photo courtesy of Romelia Boyer Schiro (Mrs. Gasper Schiro).

stage—courtesy of slide projection. And, when Moses received the tablets on Mt. Sinai, the sonorous voice of Robert Zibilich read the Ten Commandments aloud. There was a backdrop illustrating a human brain for the theme "Inner Sanctum of the Mental Realm."

For the Rossini opera *William Tell,* besides a dozen or so scene changes, there was a sixty-piece symphony orchestra and a fifty-voice chorus. Charles Cabibi, Jr., played the part of William Tell's son.

As Cabibi explained, "William Tell had to shoot the apple off my head, and it was a gold papier-mâché apple. He had an antique cross bow, with an arrow, and somebody had a string on the apple on my head so it looked like he shot it off.

"Many years later I was presented with the apple by the man who did the lights at the auditorium. He had picked it up. I still have it."

Gasper Schiro, whose father was an early member, recalled that he was sneaked in to his first event when he was only sixteen. "You really wanted to go, people wanted those invitations."

The invitations to the ball were so coveted that, according to Cabibi, it is possible that one year they were counterfeited. In 1947, when the theme concerned Noah's Ark, the rainstorm on stage was nothing compared to the tempest outside the auditorium.

In a description of the evening in Robert Tallant's book *Mardi Gras . . . As It Was*, the author recounted that the 4,700 seats on the large side of the auditorium were already filled, but there was still a crowd waiting to get in the door. "Extra police had to be summoned to prevent many from forcing their way, and then they remained at the doors, clamoring and arguing and pleading. . . . Ladies, dressed to the eyebrows, swished about furiously in their velvet and silk and taffeta, demanding of the male escorts that they 'do something.'"

There was another reason besides the performance to crave a Virgilians invitation: they had spectacular call-out favors. Cabibi noted that his father and Dr. Bertucci went to New York to find costume jewelry for the favors—and the 1953 program lists Frederick A. Wettstein as jewelers. "They did a dragon pin that was exquisite. One year they would give the necklace, the next year they would give the bracelet that matched." Not only the ladies appreciated this. "My dad had dragon cufflinks made for himself and for me," Cabibi said.

Gasper Schiro's wife, Mel, had been lent a Virgilians pin by her mother-in-law. The pin was so attractive that a fellow attendee at the Washington Mardi Gras Ball tried to rent it from her. "I said no, it belongs to my mother-in-law," Mel Schiro recounted. However, when she told the story at home, "My mother-in-law said, 'I'm giving you that piece of jewelry; it looks like you can have more fun with it than I have.'"

Mel Schiro would receive her own special favor, a gold bracelet given when she was actually the last maid in Virgilians. The krewe's final year, 1964, had as a theme "Highlights of Enchantment" and each maid and scene represented a prior ball. The last maid, Mel Schiro, represented the first ball, "Dante's Inferno."

Maids in Virgilians could expect spectacular costumes and headpieces. The late Larry Youngblood, longtime head of costumes for the New Orleans Recreation Department's theater program, had been designing for Virgilians since 1959.

As Mel Schiro described it, "I was the 'Sin of Greed' and my dress was gold satin, and covered in strings of jewels, all the way down to the floor. On my mantle were jewels, and more jewels. My headpiece was a cap, and out of the cap were big arms, one on each side, and then from the hand of one of those arms to the other were hanging necklaces of more jewels."

Why did Virgilians end? Probably there was no single reason. The ball was intricate and expensive to produce, and it required a huge commitment from members, who by that time were able to belong to other Carnival organizations. And perhaps there were so many other forms of entertainment available by the 1960s that ball-goers lacked the patience to sit through two hours of tableaux.

Like that fantastic costume, Virgilians still sparkles in the memories of its fans.

Bourbon Street Bounders

One happy Mardi Gras memory for me was the day-long parties in the French Quarter. In college, one fraternity got the L.S.U. and the Tulane chapters together each year and rented a huge space just off Bourbon Street. My husband and I were once in a group that rented the old American Legion Hall on Royal Street, now the 8th District Police Station, and had a band and lunch. That's the sort of party the Bourbon Street Bounders had, and believe me, that is one fun way to spend Carnival Day.

"Back in those days, everybody wore a costume," reminisced Mrs. Thomas Dwyer of St. Michaels, Maryland, who, under her maiden name of T. C. Larue, was formerly the society columnist for the *Times-Picayune* and can comment as a connoisseur of Mardi Gras frivolity.

Costumed uptown couples often migrated to the French Quarter on Mardi Gras Day after Rex had passed. Their destinations were parties hosted by organizations that hired a hall, offered a buffet lunch and a jazz band for dancing, with plentiful libations for the members. The three best known of such groups were the Bourbon Street Bounders, the Royal Street Rounders, and the youngest of the three, the Friars Club. None of the three is still active, nor is the Sunday Sinners, an organization that gave a popular party the Sunday before Carnival at the New Orleans Country Club.

Why were the clubs' Mardi Gras Day parties popular? "It gave you a headquarters," said T. C. Besides, you would see your friends and even be able to wander through the French Quarter until the night parade, when Comus rolled down Royal Street. Like many others, M. I. (Mrs. Guy) Scoggin recalls watching the parade uptown with her children in the morning, and then heading down past Canal Street for grown-up fun.

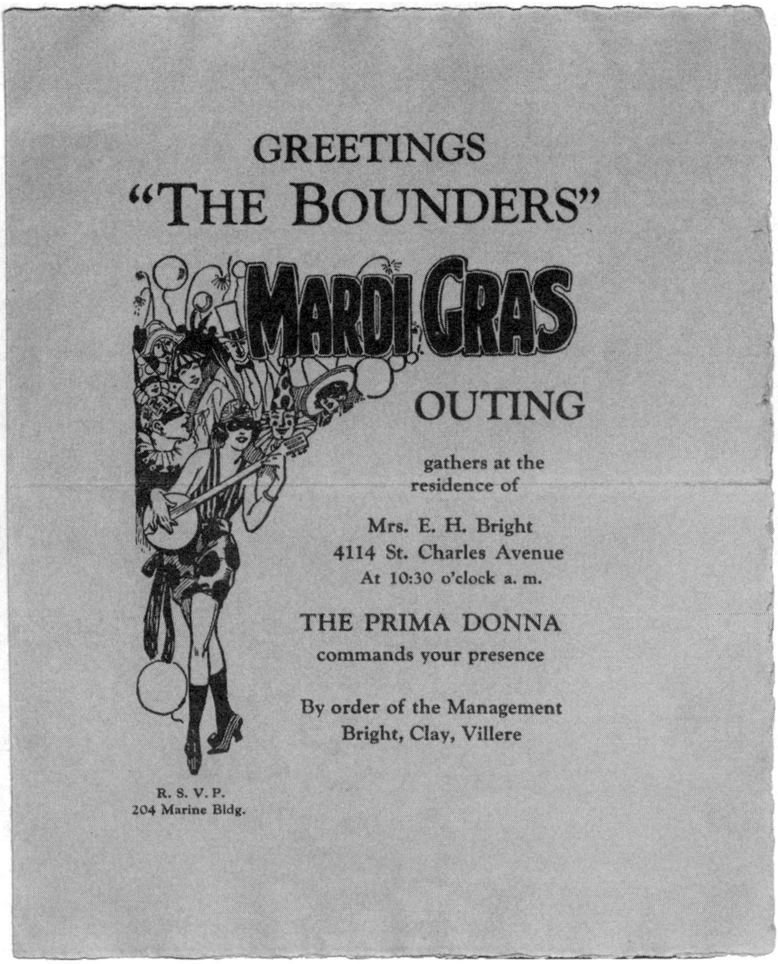

Bourbon Street Bounders invitation. Carnival Collection, Tulane University Louisiana Research Collection.

The oldest of the groups was the Bourbon Street Bounders, founded in 1919, a year no organized parades were held because of World War I. The Bounders began with a party at La Louisiane Restaurant on Iberville Street. The following year they paraded from uptown to the Quarter in a truck, and they named a king and queen, who happened to be Rex and his consort, John Clark and Elinor Bright (Mrs. Edmund) Richardson. The truck transportation was dropped, and the party location for many years was the Patio Royale, located on

Royal Street where Brennan's Restaurant is now, with the group eventually relocating to other French Quarter spots.

Getting to the French Quarter on Mardi Gras Day presented its own difficulties. Jane Shober Fox (Mrs. Richard) remembers that "it was a rat race to get to the Bounders for noon." And, besides your friends, you never knew who might turn up, including visiting celebrities. The late Esther Breckenridge, once a society reporter at the *New Orleans Item*, recalled meeting Randolph Churchill (son of Winston) at the Bounders one Carnival. Costumes were required, and were often imaginative. T. C. Larue Dwyer was costumed as Vampira the year she reigned as queen. One year a gentleman arrived in his sister's Comus maid's gown from a prior year, with the addition of an article of lingerie and a card proclaiming: "I Dreamed I Was Queen of Comus in My Maidenform Bra."

Marie (Mrs. John) McLennan ruled as queen of the Bounders one year. "How could you not have fun if you were the queen?" she noted. "We danced the whole day long, and of course you had to lead the second line, or the conga line, all through the place." The Patio Royale had a large patio area, a bar, and lots of room for dancing. The Bounders, like all the organizations, were entertained by traditional jazz bands. Papa Celestin's Orchestra, Peter Bocage's group, and Sweet Emma Barrett, "the Bell Gal," were among the bands who provided the parties' soundtracks.

The Royal Street Rounders began just after World War II and celebrated its first year at the Court of Two Sisters on Royal Street. Membership in the various organizations was somewhat fluid, and out-of-town guests were welcomed, even if they sometimes were puzzled by the experience. Marie McLellan remembered "taking somebody to the Rounders, who was from Houston, I think. He hadn't realized this was an all-day thing, and he announced he had to go to work in the middle of it!" As she recalled, "That didn't suit me at all—he just wasn't a real Mardi Gras."

Fit for a Queen: The Town and Country Shop

It used to be said that, because of Mardi Gras, New Orleans had the highest per capita champagne consumption in the country. That may or may not be true. But I would suspect that New Orleans is one of the last places where ladies might still have a pair of kid gloves, opera length (that goes all the way up your arm) in their armoire. And mine is probably not the only closet in which there are some floor-length dresses or skirts that can be brought out when needed. Mardi Gras balls require a certain wardrobe, and there are various ways of replenishing it.

In the past, the best choice was the Town and Country Shop.

"As far as I was concerned, it was 'one-stop shopping,'" Judy Walshe Whann (Mrs. Robert Whann) remembers fondly.

The Town and Country Shop, on St. Charles Avenue at Melpomene Street, was the premier dress and accessories boutique for uptown New Orleans women for most of the twentieth century. (Town and Country has moved to 1514 St. Charles Avenue, and is today under a different ownership.)

Emily Hayne Walker (Mrs. James Alexander "Dixie" Walker) was the remarkable woman who owned and presided over Town and Country for most of its existence. "Em," as she was known, had scored a unique New Orleans social double play: she was the only woman ever to reign over the krewes of both Rex (1923) and Comus (1924) (when she stood in for a sister who married in her debut year).

The 1931 New Orleans City Directory lists Emily Hayne as residing at her parents' home while being employed as a saleslady at D. H. Holmes and Company, a firm that her father served as a vice president, in addition to his ownership of a real estate company. In the 1932 directory, Emily Hayne is listed as the owner of the Town and

The Town and Country Shop, shown with Gean and Jesse Thornburg, who purchased it in the 1980s. Photo courtesy of Jesse Thornburg.

Country Shop, located at 1432 St. Charles Avenue, which would be its address for over half a century of her personal oversight.

The women who worked at Town and Country were often from uptown families and were convivial as well as knowledgeable. Mrs. Whann's mother, the late Katie Walshe (Mrs. William Walshe), spent a career at Town and Country—she had first had a children's shop, with a partner, then Town and Country absorbed it as the children's department, and "then she worked there with the regular shop."

Susan Jones Gundlach (Mrs. James Gundlach) admitted that the store was "pretty much where I bought my clothes." She also remembered that "at 5 o'clock, some of the ladies who worked there would have their little cocktail."

Town and Country was a party place, in many ways.

The late Louise Reiss Rogas (Mrs. Gene Rogas) had a long career at Town and Country, and is best remembered as a particularly discerning buyer on her trips to New York to stock the racks with gowns. When she came in 1959, she had no retail experience. "I think Emily took me on 'spec,'" she admitted when I interviewed her in 2008. "In fact, I had just come home from Washington and I had worked for the Central Intelligence Agency for five years."

Perhaps her espionage background came in handy at Carnival—"we had to know the queens ahead of time," Mrs. Rogas recalled. Town and Country at one time had seamstresses who made bridal gowns and queens' dresses, and when they focused on ready-to-wear, the shop still fitted gowns. "We did whole balls, we always did Osiris," she recalled.

Bessie Derby Miller (Mrs. Stephen Miller of Baltimore) was a maid in Osiris and was fitted for her gown at Town and Country. Besides clothes, Mrs. Miller credited Town and Country with imparting important knowledge. "They would help you with your curtsey, and how you held yourself in the gown," she said. "Your confidence was impacted, too."

Evening gowns were an important part of Town and Country's allure. As Mrs. Rogas noted, "We did an enormous debutante business; in fact we carried more individual debutante dresses than any store in the United States—because we could only have one of each."

Town and Country buyers searched out those racks of white dresses. "We were extremely well known in that market in New York. A lot of the gowns were from bridal houses but many of them were from expensive evening houses. We carried more than Neiman Marcus or Saks," Mrs. Rogas said.

She credits the shop's success to its wide range of merchandise. "It was a broad brush—we covered everything from children to old ladies." Some boutiques today might have "a few lines (of dresses) in depth, but we must have carried two hundred different lines. It was a big broad spectrum, from inexpensive to expensive, from ball gowns to sportswear. We even had stockings."

You could buy baby gifts, decorative items, purses. And, best of all, you could shop at the summer and winter sales.

"They were legendary. People used to line up around the corner. It was hilarious," Mrs. Rogas said. And the sales' popularity was well deserved: "We really gave everybody a good buy and the clothes were wonderful, innovative things."

The sales were also a good marketing tool: "We never lost any money on sales, and we sure got some stuff out of there," Mrs. Rogas said. "We had people who only shopped with us twice a year, but boy, they bought!"

Unique clothes, good value, personal attention: all added up to Town and Country's mystique. Kit Wisdom remembered being at a Town and Country sale with a friend, tossing things over the dressing room walls to each other and hearing nearby a plaintive voice inquire: "Is it all right for somebody who is thirty-two to wear a sleeveless dress?" and Em Walker answering, "Of course it is!" "We laughed over that for years—we were about twenty-two back then," Ms. Wisdom said.

Customers at Town and Country were catered to—and if something didn't fit properly (sleeveless or not) you could always have it altered. With a Mrs. Royals at the head, it was the "most fabulous alterations department in town," according to Mrs. Rogas. "They could do anything. Those women knew how to sew, and fit. They fit all the debs. Some customers wouldn't let another soul touch their clothes." The alterations department could work wonders, but "that one we never made any money on—it was a service, a real service."

One dressmaking innovation that began at Town and Country was the use of a back brace device to help Carnival queens hold up their heavy collars and mantles—a young monarch injured in a riding accident made the suggestion.

It was the personal service that marked Town and Country. Mrs. Whann noted that "during debuts, they all helped. They had seen my daughter grow up. It was just like one big family." Em Walker herself was a draw: "You want to see the owner when you go in, it really makes a difference," according to Mrs. Gundlach.

"Everybody would call me by name, and would remember the colors I liked, and the kinds of things I liked," noted Kit Wisdom, "or somebody would call and say we've put something aside for you."

Adelaide Wisdom Benjamin (Mrs. Edward Benjamin) remembered that "what I loved the best—they had this big room, the farthest away from the front door. And, it had triple mirrors and several chairs, a place for my mother to watch while I tried on dresses. Em would sit and talk to us, and she knew everything in her shop—she'd say 'get that pale lavender' and they would get it and it would be perfect!"

After Em died in 1986 the shop went out of her family. Then, Jesse Thornburg and his late wife, Gean, owners of a popular dress shop in Mandeville, took over Town and Country, and eventually moved it to the next block of St. Charles.

Louise Rogas cherished fond memories. Working at Town and Country "could be anything you wanted it to be," she said. Besides being a buyer (along with her friends the late Dolly Ann Souchon Johnsen and Mickey Dureau and Patty O'Brien), she pitched in to dress the windows and write the advertising.

"I never took a vacation, I absolutely loved that business," she said.

Mardi Gras Ball Music: The Big Band Sound

THE BIG MARDI GRAS BALLS, especially in the old-line krewes, always depend on a dance band, actually an orchestra, for their music. After the dancing begins, you hear a special bouncy beat that seems to vaguely satisfy all ages of dancers. If you make it to a number of balls, and you have the occasional big debutante party in a given year, you get accustomed to that year's favorite tunes. Plus, there are always New Orleans dance standards: that can vary from "Stardust" to the Meters's "They All Ask'd for You."

One of my longtime favorite bands was René Louapre's. I knew someone in the band who worked at WDSU-TV when I did, so I felt I had a friend on stage. We never had a signature song he would play for us, but I did know someone who always got "Tea for Two" when that couple reached the dance floor.

The René Louapre Society Orchestra was a mainstay of the New Orleans Carnival season for most of the twentieth century. His son Henri Louapre pointed out that "my Dad played for fifty Comuses. He even had a specially made gold tails jacket he wore just for that."

René Louapre died in 1987 at the age of seventy-one. He was a 1932 graduate of Warren Easton High School and a 1933 graduate of Jesuit High School (according to his son, the sixteen-year-old was a little young for college, and since Jesuit needed a trumpet player that year, he managed to get two high school diplomas). A music degree from Loyola University followed, and he received a master's in music from Northwestern University in Evanston, Illinois. Ultimately, the senior Louapre spent thirty-two years working for the Orleans Parish Public Schools, most notably as supervisor of instrumental music. "That was when all the schools had orchestras—not just bands," according to Henri.

René Louapre, in a 1984 interview with *All Right*, a WWOZ-

Top: Jimmy Maxwell conducting his orchestra at a Mardi Gras ball. Photo courtesy of Jimmy Maxwell.
Bottom: The Jimmy Maxwell Orchestra. Photo courtesy of Jimmy Maxwell.

FM radio magazine, said he had his first trumpet lesson at the age of ten, and soon was playing cornet with the Sons of Firemen, who gave him a free horn. He had some private music lessons, played in school, and after he had a full-time job, he kept playing at night. He was soon playing regularly with the Leslie George Orchestra, which provided music for many of the old-line Carnival krewes. After Mardi Gras went on hiatus during World War II (which René spent in the U.S. Army), Leslie George left the city. René Louapre picked up the baton and his Society Orchestra began playing for balls and other events. Soon, as many as forty Carnival balls might be on the Louapre calendar.

Meanwhile, he kept up with his day job and the family grew. As son Henri explained, "It's a difficult life when you're trying to work in the day and play music till four o'clock in the morning.

"It was hard. I never spent a New Year's Eve with my father, because he always played—the New Orleans Country Club," Henri Louapre admitted.

Cecilia Wark Louapre took on the responsibility of raising the family. The Louapre clan ultimately included five children: Kathleen (Howell), Cecilia (Taylor), Dr. René Louapre III, Margaret (Arnold), and Henri ("the caboose"), currently chairman of the Loubat Equipment Company. Kathleen graduated from Dominican College—the rest graduated, like their father, from Loyola University.

The Louapre family didn't listen to music at home, and their mother did not play. The children all took lessons. The girls played in the band at Dominican High School. René III was the only one who joined his father as a musician on stage, but Henri helped his father with management and travel details as the years went on.

After all those social occasions and music, René Louapre's concept of the ideal vacation atmosphere was peace and quiet. As Henri remembered, "When we were very small we would go travelling. We would go up to Montana and Canada. He drove. We all had assigned seats, and the car was a '57 Plymouth. We loaded it up, and went. One year we drove all the way up to Lake Louise, in Canada."

The leader was not the only one working two jobs in Louapre's orchestra, which usually had fourteen or so members. In a 1968 interview for *New Orleans* magazine, René listed some of his musicians' other occupations: saxophonist Jim Rush was the traffic manager at WDSU-TV, Lloyd Daigle played guitar and was a pharmacist at Maison Blanche, trombonist Angelo Castigliola worked at Woodward Wight.

While he could take a summer off from his two occupations, René Louapre's orchestra might not get a regular break on the bandstand, playing nonstop through an event. This style of playing became fashionable in the postwar era through New York bandleader Lester Lanin.

According to Jimmy Maxwell, son of Louapre's drummer Eddie Maxwell, and now leader of the Jimmy Maxwell Orchestra, Lester Lanin once played a job at the New Orleans Country Club. Louapre heard him, and picked up on the popularity of nonstop music. Lanin's "businessman's bounce" was not far from Louapre's cheerful one-step.

René Louapre commented in 1968 that the one-step was the ideal beat for call-out dances since the krewe members might get drowsy in their restrictive masks and need a little energizing on the dance floor. "We save the dreamy, slow romantic ballads for the dancing after the call-outs."

According to Maxwell, and to Louapre in his 1968 interview, the pattern for music at carnival balls still involves hard work for the band members. There might be a small group playing for the krewe members before the ball, then the ball begins with march music (the Triumphal March from *Aida,* the Coronation March from *Le Prophète,* and, for Rex, "If Ever I Cease to Love"). Suitable music for the tableaux follows—whether classical or show tunes, it is carefully orchestrated and timed to suit the performance—and then music for dancing. The band might play another four hours for the queen's supper or the supper dance following the ball.

As René Louapre noted in 1968, the goal of the orchestra is to get happy dancers out on the floor. "Music must make people happy—it's an emotional healer as well as a business."

As Jimmy Maxwell pointed out, "The aim is to see how many people you can get on the dance floor."

Maxwell himself was once part of the Louapre Orchestra, and now his own son, Robert Maxwell, is conducting. In all those years, the musicians have continually adapted popular tunes. As Maxwell explained, "Under René Louapre, you might play 'In the Mood,' 'Mack the Knife,' and 'New York, New York'; later on 'Brown-Eyed Girl' was popular.

"Nowadays we might play 'Forget You' by Cee Lo Green, or 'Rehab' by Amy Winehouse," Maxwell said.

René Louapre used to occasionally play a favorite tune of someone on the dance floor. Jimmy Maxwell noted that "older people, some still have signature songs. I will squeeze their song in, they will look up, there's an acknowledgment."

Today, Jimmy Maxwell's orchestra often plays in other cities. Louapre's orchestra traveled too, but not as extensively. Maxwell has a more national focus since he was in business with New York orchestra leader Peter Duchin for some years.

The makeup of groups has changed, too. "Sometimes I bring down musicians from New York, guys I knew with Duchin's band. If you're playing a party in Atlanta, you may have a bass player from Chicago."

Like René Louapre in his later years, Maxwell fields orchestras for both the Rex and Comus balls. Louapre always was at Comus, but for some years the Harry Morel Orchestra played for Rex.

You can check the Jimmy Maxwell Orchestra (JMO) on Facebook or go to jimmymaxwellorchestra.com, for his plans this year, but as Maxwell explained, most Mardi Gras nights "there will be two fourteen- or fifteen-piece orchestras. I am responsible for both. I'm there for the beginning of Rex, I then turn over the conducting, and then I reappear across the street for the beginning of Comus, and I see Comus through to the end of the night."

Or, until the last dancer leaves the floor.

Glad-U-Kum to Mardi Gras: The Jerusalem Temple

For years, the big Mardi Gras balls were held in the Municipal Auditorium on Rampart Street. When the auditorium closed and was used as a casino until Harrah's moved to Canal Street, ball-goers became accustomed to going to hotels. In my opinion, since sometimes they serve refreshments to the audience, the hotels were, and still are, acceptable substitutes. The auditorium, meanwhile, was damaged badly in Katrina and has not been rebuilt.

However, there were always a few balls that picked another spot for the event. And one of the possible spots was the conveniently located Jerusalem Temple on St. Charles Avenue just above Lee Circle. I recall going to balls upstairs in the auditorium and also some events on the ground floor. Although it no longer hosts balls today, in the past the Jerusalem Temple had much to recommend it.

"The best part was riding down St. Charles Avenue in the limousines right after the Hermes parade. That was really fun!" Judy Walshe Whann (Mrs. Robert Whann) was remembering her reign over the youthful Krewe of Apollo on the Friday before Mardi Gras. Her ride up the avenue stopped short of Lee Circle. In those years, Apollo and a high school girls' krewe, Les Pierrettes, held balls at the Jerusalem Temple building.

The Jerusalem Temple had an auditorium suitable for Carnival balls, plus a large room on the ground floor that could also be used for dances. As you entered, you could read an intriguing sign: Glad-U-Kum. The sentiment was kindly meant, and the pseudo-Arabic spelling was dear to the hearts of the building's owners, the Shriners.

For some years now, the building, on St. Charles Avenue at the corner of Clio Street, has been occupied by a church, but it is best known as an oddity when glimpsed from a streetcar window. The design owes much to the Middle East, not usually an inspiring source

The Jerusalem Temple building, now housing a church, St. Charles Avenue at Clio Street. Photo by Carolyn Kolb.

for local architects. But Emile Weil, who designed this circa-1920 edifice, had as his clients a local chapter of the group called the Ancient Arabic Order of the Nobles of the Mystic Shrine (A.A.O.N.M.S.), and he delivered just what they wanted. We know them as the Shriners.

Shrine members are Masons, and are proud of their long tradition of communal activities and ritual. New York Masons founded the Shriners in 1872, with the idea that the new group would focus on fun and philanthropy, with a Middle Eastern slant. Officers were Nobles or Potentates, chapters were to be called Temples, and the group used Arabic emblems (members wear a fez, a flowerpot-like Moroccan hat) and language (Shriners might salute each other by saying, "Es Selamu Aleikum!"—meaning "Peace be with you!").

Jerusalem Temple in New Orleans was granted its charter in 1888, and by 1910 was hosting the thirty-sixth annual session of the Imperial Council. Future plans for building the local temple were outlined in the program of the council, and by the 1920s the Jerusalem Temple was open.

The auditorium inside was a popular spot for visiting performers. In 1925 Paul Whiteman and his orchestra played there, under the auspices of Werlein's music store. Whiteman's program proclaimed that "the greatest single factor in the improvement of American popular music" was his setting orchestral arrangements for "that blatant method of treating music" that "came to be known as jazz."

The actress Eleonore Duse brought her troupe with her from Rome, ballerina Anna Pavlova and her corps de ballet performed an eclectic program including "California Poppy" and "Krishna's Wedding." Monologist Ruth Draper took the stage, as did motivational speaker Emile Coué.

Jessie Tharp presented the Abbey Theatre Irish Players, the National Theater of the Irish Free State, in 1932. Actor Barry Fitzgerald starred in *Juno and the Paycock* by Sean O'Casey and *The Playboy of the Western World* by J. M. Synge.

The Jerusalem Temple served the entire community, at a time when some venues were not open to all races. African American soprano Dorothy Maynor had previously appeared before a small crowd at Dillard University, but, according to the *Louisiana Weekly*, the "better seating" at the Jerusalem Temple meant that patrons should purchase tickets to fill the hall "even if it means a personal sacrifice." Endorsing organizations of the event included the B Sharp Music Club, the Urban League, the NAACP, and also the music department of Newcomb College, Le Petit Theatre du Vieux Carré, and the Philharmonic Society of New Orleans.

An auditorium that could host such performances was obviously well suited for a tradition of Carnival activities, as Alan Smason can attest.

Smason has had a lifelong relationship with the Jerusalem Temple. "I still keep up my membership as a Shriner," he said, and his late father, optometrist Arnold Smason, served a year as Potentate (president) of the Temple.

The night before he was born, Alan's mother, Annette Smason, was there, "dancing at the Moslem Ball." Moslem was a krewe with

Shriners as members. Shriners also sponsored a women's krewe, Noblads ("the NOBles' LADies"). Moslem would merge into Mecca and then into the Knights of Sparta, according to Smason.

Family connections to Jerusalem Temple were strong. Alan's grandfather had a drugstore next to the building, but moved up the avenue next to the Pontchartrain Hotel, and his mother, Annette, operated Smith's Record Shop adjacent to the drugstore. His mother celebrated both her fifth and her fiftieth birthday with parties at the Jerusalem Temple, and she was a longtime member of the Krewe of Venus. ("The year my father was Potentate, my mother was Queen of Venus," Smason noted.)

Smason's own interest in Mardi Gras includes writing scripts and narrating balls and parades. Groups he has served include krewes of Okeanos, Iris, Carrollton, Thoth, Babylon, Mid-City, Venus, Knights of Sparta, Zeus, Pandora, and Freret.

Mardi Gras days at the Temple were a big event. "You could go inside for a hotdog, and when you came out, there was Mardi Gras, right there!" Smason recalled. One year he and his late wife, Sally, had such good costumes ("I went as a Smurf!") that only a lot of convincing could get them inside for the Shriners' party.

Uptown high schoolers might have been to dances downstairs at the Jerusalem Temple, but when Apollo and Les Pierrettes had balls, the action was in the auditorium.

Betty Anne Gordon (Mrs. John A. Gordon) served as longtime chairman of Les Pierrettes, which had a limited membership. "The most you could have at the Jerusalem Temple, according to the fire marshall, was two hundred members." She still recalls with pleasure her krewe members: "They were so young and fresh, it was so nice to see it through their eyes—they were just delighted with themselves."

At every ball the female krewe members would look out nervously over the auditorium. "The boys would stay in the hallways. There would be nobody in the call-out seats and the girls would say, 'Nobody came!' But then, when the lights went down, you could see all these black tuxedoed figures," Mrs. Gordon remembered. "I think Perlis's men's shop loved us—the boys were all growing so fast, none of them owned his own tuxedo and they all had to rent one!"

The Jerusalem Temple today is owned by the Church of the King, a Mandeville congregation. The Jerusalem Temple Shriners have headquarters in Destrehan. There is still a Shrine Circus annual fundraiser (Alan Smason's father became friends with aerialist Karl Wallenda over years of working to bring the circus here) and Shriners still have their clown units, motorcycles, and funny cars.

There are 400,000 Shriners throughout the United States, Canada, Mexico, and the Republic of Panama. There are twenty-two Shriners Hospitals for Children providing care for orthopedic conditions, burns, spinal cord injuries, and cleft lip and palate. These hospitals have helped some 835,000 children—at no cost to parent or child—since the first Shriners hospital opened in 1922.

And, to add to their other good deeds, the Shriners have left some fond Mardi Gras memories.

The Mardi Gras Coalition

If I had to pick one pivotal Mardi Gras, it would have to be the one right after the 1969 film *Easy Rider*. Granted, the French Quarter is always going to be crowded at Carnival time, and young people were expected to join in. But no one could have predicted the huge numbers of kids who turned up.

The plot of Peter Fonda's hip epic had to do with young motorcycle riders, a narcotics deal, and a trip to Mardi Gras.

In *Easy Rider*, the sequence filmed in St. Louis Number 1 Cemetery is the one that most of us remember best.

Dennis Hopper and Peter Fonda, accompanied by two ladies of the evening, Karen Black and Toni Basil, wander among the tombs, take some LSD, and generally cavort au naturel. (If you were wondering, the same Toni Basil had a hit song, "Mickey," in 1982—and she still works as a choreographer and appears in commercials.) From the looks of the finished product, cast and crew were striving for cinema verité.

Les Blank, an acclaimed documentary maker with many local ties, shot the cemetery sequence and never received credit for it. Poignantly, the whole sequence is punctuated by the sound of the pile drivers putting in the elevated expressway along North Claiborne Avenue that destroyed the oak-lined heart of the black Seventh Ward community the route bisects. And, if you look closely in the Mardi Gras sequences, you will see the Krewe of Proteus's night parade through the streets of the French Quarter, one of the last years that route was followed.

The immediate effect of the release of *Easy Rider* in 1969 was the influx of young people who arrived the following year to attend what was then billed as "The Greatest Free Show on Earth"—Mardi Gras. While some of us noticed the cemetery scene, the rest of the country

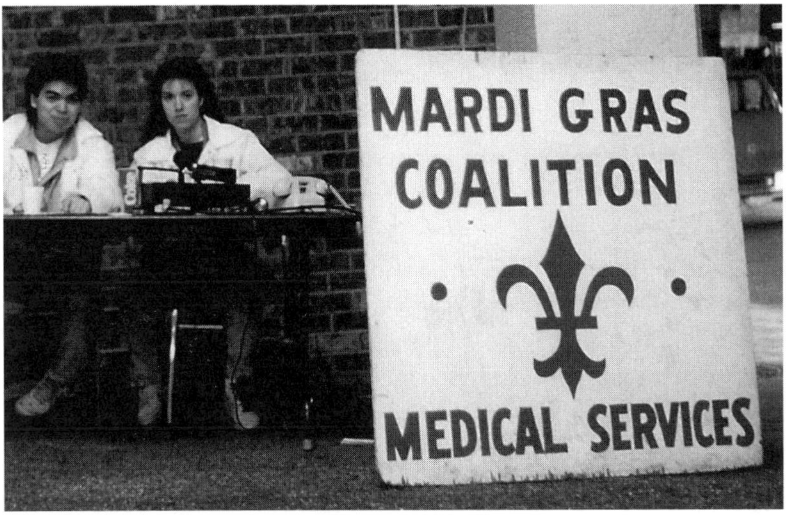

The Mardi Gras Coalition, student workers. Photo courtesy of CACTUS Record Group, Mardi Gras Coalition Scrapbook, University Archives, Tulane University.

was enthralled by the Mardi Gras parade and crowd shots (actually filmed in 16mm the prior year and spliced into the movie). Apparently they all thought, Wow! I want to go THERE!

The effect the first year was immediate: young people were sleeping in the parks, crashing in doorways, overdosing and overdrinking and overexposing themselves, and generally partying themselves into an unmanageable mass that filled up the Quarter and spilled over into the rest of the city.

Attorney Gideon Stanton remembers being on a talk show with a prominent local businessman, with the third guest being a retired conservative politician from the Northeast.

The talk show host asked: what are we going to do about all these Mardi Gras visitors? Stanton ventured the opinion that calling the holiday the "Greatest Free Show on Earth" was taken seriously and the city just had to make them welcome. The local businessman declared that all Mardi Gras visitors should be checked at the city limits to see if they had enough money to cover their expenses and refused entry if they didn't. The northerner pointed out the obvious: that was an absurd suggestion; you just can't do that.

What evolved to tackle the problem was the Mardi Gras Coalition—an alliance of charitable and student organizations, doctors, and lawyers, who banded together with the administration of Mayor Moon Landrieu and the police chief (both Joseph Giarrusso and Clarence Giarrusso in turn).

The coalition's objective was to adequately handle the influx of penniless young people, see that they had a safe experience, and absorb them into the celebration without changing Mardi Gras for locals and other visitors. The idea caught on: an early volunteer was the daughter of the businessman who had advocated closing the borders.

Gideon Stanton was a student at Tulane Law School when the late Donald Mintz gave him responsibility for setting up a student community service organization Mintz had found some university funds to support. Stanton, along with the late Bill Hill, an African American student at Tulane, wrote a grant application to the Stern Family Fund and got funding to run the Community Activities Committee of Tulane University Students—CACTUS—for three years. Stanton became the organization's executive director, with a salary paid jointly by the university and by the student council. "In those days the students and the university could hardly agree on anything, and since they would both have had to approve firing me, I had job security," Stanton laughs.

As Stanton recalls, there was an incident when two out-of-town college girls were mauled by a police dog sent in to check the hovel where they had their sleeping bags. In town for Carnival, they had nowhere to stay.

Tulane students were aroused and wanted to do something. CACTUS came up with an idea. "We had some emergency medicine instructors come on campus and train students, and we would send them out in the Quarter to give aid where they could," he added. Some of those student volunteers later became doctors, and, in one case, they were credited with saving the life of a reveler who fell from a balcony.

Meanwhile, other organizations were moving, on their own, to do something to help the visitors. "It just built in layers," Stanton said. Soon the overall coordinating organization would be called the Mardi Gras Coalition. The late Mike Stark, a gay activist in the Quarter who had been a minister and became a mask maker, served as chairman of the coalition one year. The late Bill Rushton, a young architect and journalist, was chairman another year.

One of the main Mardi Gras Coalition activities was production of a Mardi Gras survival booklet for visitors. "Welcome, brothers and sisters," it begins, and notes, "May your experience here be creative and peaceful." The rest of the book lists the services available: temporary housing at St. Mark's Community Center on Rampart Street, the Head Inn on Decatur Street, charging "$1.00 for floor crash," plus what housing was available at the Salvation Army, Ozanam Inn, and Baptist Rescue Mission, medical help at the Head Clinic—run with volunteer medical help—Charity Hospital, and the City Venereal Disease Clinic. Even cheap places to eat were listed: Buster Holmes had red beans for lunch and a sixty-cent breakfast, Roma Restaurant on Decatur had a one-dollar plate lunch, some missions served free meals. The Process on Ursuline Street ran a free store and served free meals. And still the young people poured into town.

"There were so many people who showed up on campus that the administration let us open Tulane Stadium for them," Stanton remembered. One of the problems the coalition solved was the lack of bathrooms. "Tony Gagliano was in the mayor's office and he helped us get some donated Port-O-Lets. We chose the locations for them around the French Quarter," Stanton added.

Another important activity of the coalition was legal aid: Tulane law students, cooperating attorneys from the American Civil Liberties Union, volunteers who did pro bono work from their practices—there were plenty of problems to solve. "Marijuana use was a state offense," Stanton recalled. Those arrested might also face fees from bail bondsmen. Stanton remembers meeting with Criminal Sheriff Charles Foti to work out some solutions. The coalition handbook devoted space to warnings on how to avoid confrontations with the law, and what to do if arrested.

The Mardi Gras Coalition continued through the early 1970s, and gradually a routine was set. "Each year we would start it up, contact all the parties, schedule the meetings," Stanton remembers. Slowly the numbers of young visitors dropped to a manageable level. "Eventually the need for it dissipated," Stanton said of the coalition.

Today Tulane still has CACTUS, and the Tulane Emergency

Medical Service counts the coalition as its founding impetus. There are still youth service centers in and near the French Quarter, and perhaps what we now refer to as the homeless at Mardi Gras time are not much different from the young hippies who made this their party.

But if they get in St. Louis Number 1, let's hope they keep their clothes on—at least while the cameras are on them.

Mardi Gras Bibliography

No need to be hemmed in by the calendar when it comes to celebrating Mardi Gras—what with music, videos, and even the proper liquid refreshment, you can celebrate Carnival all year round.

First Things First

If you really want to get in the Mardi Gras mood, make yourself a Hurricane—passion fruit punch and lots of rum—as served at Pat O'Brien's bar on St. Peter Street just off Bourbon Street. Maybe it's not something anyone would drink every day—but then it's Carnival time!

Hurricane Drink Mix, available at Patobriens.com

Mardi Gras Videos

You can't just talk about Mardi Gras—you have to *show* it. These documentaries tell different Mardi Gras stories, and each has its own special feel about an aspect of the celebration.

Gay Mardi Gras is triumphantly outrageous, but life, and celebration, have not always been easy to navigate for this important segment of the New Orleans population. This video tells their story.

The Sons of Tennessee Williams. 2011. Written, produced, directed, and edited by Tim Wolff; director of photography, Eric Adkin. First Run Features.

The African American community of New Orleans, especially in the city's Seventh Ward, have their own Mardi Gras traditions and costuming customs. This video is a tribute to those memories, and a look at current celebrations.

All on a Mardi Gras Day. 2003. Written and directed by Royce Osborn, produced by Jerry Brock and Royce Osborn. Spyboy Pictures.

The Mardi Gras Indians, a fixture in Mardi Gras history, have pride in their traditions and an important role in the African American community's Mardi Gras. Focusing on Yellow Pocahontas Chief Tootie Montana, this video captures the Mardi Gras Indian spirit.

Tootie's Last Suit. Lisa Katzman. 2009. Pomegranate Productions.

A very personal look at white society's Mardi Gras traditions, this thoughtful documentary tells the story of a young woman born into that milieu, and her experiences.

By Invitation Only. Rebecca Snedeker. 2006. Palmetto Pictures.

A debutante, an exotic dancer, a Mardi Gras Indian, a gay man mourning a friend: four different stories of Mardi Gras combine in this film.

Cutting Loose. Andrew Young and Susan Todd. 1995. Chantal Bernheim for Leapfrog/DUNE.

Cajun country Mardi Gras is a party on horseback—and this look at the celebration is both joyous and remarkable.

Dance for a Chicken. Pat Mire. 1993. Eunice, La.: Attakapas Productions.

The filmmaker who contributed the Mardi Gras and cemetery sequences to the smash hit *Easy Rider* has focused his documentary lens on other facets of Mardi Gras.

Always for Pleasure. Les Blank. 1978. Flower Films.

If you still want more Mardi Gras, do what Orleanians do: get a copy of this year's grand finale and curl up at home to watch.

Rex Ball and Meeting of the Courts of Rex and Comus. WYES-TV (available at wyes.org).

Mardi Gras Books

No one should go through Mardi Gras without a copy of *Arthur Hardy's Mardi Gras Guide*. Hardy began as a Carnival fan, but he has made himself into the preeminent authority on the subject. A little history, a lot of information, necessary logistics: Hardy's guide is a necessity for parade-goers.

Hardy, Arthur, 2012. *Arthur Hardy's 2012 Mardi Gras Guide*. New Orleans: Arthur Hardy Enterprises, Inc. (published every year, available online at mardigrasguide.com).

Carnival history, mostly of the society celebration, has been a fascinating topic in the city for years. The older books (Tallant, La Cour, and Young) are interesting, but a more tempered and comprehensive view can be found in the two recent works by Errol Laborde. For a glorious salute to early Mardi Gras, swoon over the beautiful artwork in Schindler's collection of ball invitation reproductions.

Laborde, Errol. 2007. *Krewe: The Early New Orleans Carnival, Comus to Zulu*. Metairie, La.: Carnival Press.

———. 1999. *Marched the Day God: A History of the Rex Organization*. New Orleans, La.: School of Design.

La Cour, Arthur, in collaboration with Stuart Omer Landry. 1952. *New Orleans Masquerade: Chronicles of Carnival*. Gretna, La.: Pelican Publishing Company.

Schindler, Henri. 2000. *Mardi Gras Treasures: Invitations of the Golden Age*. New Orleans, La.: Pelican Publications.

Tallant, Robert. 1948. *Mardi Gras*. New York: Doubleday and Company.

Young, Perry. 1931. *The Mistick Krewe: Chronicles of Comus and His Kin*. New Orleans, La.: Carnival Press.

Two more Mardi Gras titles will view Carnival from a different angle, and give a contemporary perspective.

Gill, James. 1997. *Lords of Misrule: Mardi Gras and the Politics of Race in New Orleans.* Jackson, Miss.: University Press of Mississippi.
Mitchell, Reid. 1995. *All on a Mardi Gras Day: Episodes in the History of New Orleans Carnival.* Cambridge, Mass.: Harvard University Press.

Mardi Gras Music

This is New Orleans, after all, and you can't have a Mardi Gras without music. Everybody is going to have favorite tunes and performers, but this list should have a little something for everyone (and would sound just right if you are having a Mardi Gras party of your own).

First, go online and stream music from WWOZ.org. WWOZ is a New Orleans public radio station that is a treasure trove of local music. Do this on Mardi Gras day, crank up the volume, and it's an instant party.

The theme song of the Rex Organization, and the Mardi Gras anthem, is "If Ever I Cease to Love." The song started out as a sort of vaudeville novelty number, supposedly a favorite of performer Lydia Thompson, whose biggest fan was the Grand Duke Alexis of Russia, a sensation himself as a guest in New Orleans in the 1870s. Doesn't make much sense, but this is Mardi Gras. The best version of the song is the one by Dr. Edmond Souchon, a jazz fan and musician, and a devoted member of the Rex Organization (his miniature Rex floats used to be displayed in the Rex Room at Antoine's Restaurant). Doc's gravelly voice, as he and the rest of Johnny Wiggs's band provide accompaniment, strikes just the right nostalgic note. You can find this tune on an album with other traditional Mardi Gras jazz pieces you will definitely enjoy.

Mardi Gras Parade Music From New Orleans. GHB Records, available at jazzology.com.

Traditional Mardi Gras ball music, with its operatic marches and fanfares, and its somewhat predictable tunes for the evening's dancing, is usually only available to hear in person. The resourceful Jimmy Maxwell, whose orchestra provides much of that music every season, has an online album re-creating a Mardi Gras ball. If you want to know what one sounds like, try downloading this.

At the Mardi Gras Ball. Jimmy Maxwell Orchestra, available for download on iTunes. Go to Jimmymaxwell.com, or, on Facebook, JMO-Jimmy Maxwell & His Orchestra.

Picking your favorite Mardi Gras songs is a conversational time passer with the same likelihood of varying answers as naming the seven dwarves. Somewhere there is a correct list, but everybody is going to have his or her own opinion. (Hint: Funky ought to be one of the seven. . . .) Here is my version of the favorite Mardi Gras song list. Rhythm and blues dominates, with an emphasis on that special New Orleans almost-Latin beat, and a few new favorites add some spice.

These records are my personal choices. You can dance, you can sing along (maybe "throw my baby out the window, let the joint burn down" in "Carnival Time" is a best-ever lyric), and when you hear them, you know there's a parade coming!

Carnival Time, Al Johnson.
How important was this song to the artist? He now calls himself Al "Carnival Time" Johnson.

Go to the Mardi Gras, Professor Longhair.
The essential New Orleans piano player. Wait for the whistled solo!

They All Ask'd for You, The Meters. So perfect it became an instant traditional folk song.

Mardi Gras Mambo, The Hawkettes. One of those songs that you can't get out of your head. Mambo Mambo Mambo, etc.

Mardi Gras Indians have their own traditional music, their own parading customs, and their own language (probably with a little Creole French mixed in). It all translates well into New Orleans Mardi Gras classics.

Jock-A-Mo, Sugar Boy Crawford and His Cane Cutters
Iko Iko, Dixie Cups
New Suit, The Wild Magnolias
Hey Pocky-A-Way and *Fire on the Bayou,* The Meters
Big Chief Part 1 and 2, Professor Longhair

The New Orleans traditional brass band was always an essential part of Mardi Gras (you can hear one on the band wagon in the Rex parade) and the new, funkier brass bands' sound works well at Carnival, too. The two tunes have the best of both worlds.

Do Watcha Wanna, Rebirth Brass Band (contemporary)
Little Liza Jane, Dejan's Olympia Brass Band (traditional)
Second Line, Stop, Inc. (great modern version of a familiar parade song)

Here are two CDs to order that will satisfy your Mardi Gras needs, and include some earlier recordings. You can order from LouisianaMusicFactory.com (or buy your own from them at 210 Decatur Street in the French Quarter). This website has eighty-two entries in the Mardi Gras music category.

Mardi Gras in New Orleans, 1989, Mardi Gras Records
Best of Mardi Gras in New Orleans, Vol. 2, 1995, Mardi Gras Records

PART THREE

Literature

New Orleans, as a setting or as a topic, has never left any writer at a loss for words. Probably since my earliest days, lying on the floor looking at the Young People's Page in the *Times-Picayune,* I have been reading things written in or about this city. It is endlessly fascinating to me and, obviously, to a number of writers who keep churning out more pages about it.

New Orleans has long thrived on its image as a city where drinking, racy possibilities of entertainment, and a lush European look all combine to produce a place where tourists might find an out-of-the-ordinary experience. Long before the "what happens here, stays here" rationale fueled Las Vegas's tourism industry, New Orleans welcomed its own atypical civic picture. And it paid off in revenue over the years. But does that reflect reality? Well, it depends.

Yes, New Orleans is a lovely city with lush vegetation and a stock of nineteenth-century buildings serving as a backdrop to a vibrant cultural scene, with music and art and frantic sports fans and good food and unbelievable civic festivals.

But New Orleans is also a poor city, with crime, a record of political shenanigans, and latent racial tensions, surrounded by water (river and lake and swamp) and at the mercy of natural disasters.

Obviously, with all those facts in view, New Orleans is both a marvelous topic for writers and a great place for writers to work.

I can say that honestly, because I still enjoy reading about New Orleans, I am a writer myself, and I work here.

I have been a writer since I was twelve and published a story about John James Audubon in the magazine of the Children of the American Revolution. (I still have friends from my days as a member of New Orleans's Bienville C.A.R. chapter.) Once, I entered a poetry contest and had a poem hung on the fence at Jackson Square.

I wrote for my high school newspaper and for the *Bogalusa Daily News.* I wrote for the *Hullabaloo* at Tulane while I was at Newcomb, and after I graduated I worked as a city desk reporter at the *Times-Picayune*.

I was a stringer (part-time correspondent) for Reuters, British News Service, and I covered District Attorney Jim Garrison's unsuccessful (and totally unfounded in my view) case against Clay Shaw for conspiring to assassinate President John F. Kennedy.

I wrote a guidebook to New Orleans for Doubleday Publishing Company (*New Orleans: An Invitation to Discover One of America's Most Fascinating Cities*) and rewrote it as the *Dolphin Guide to New Orleans* for the 1984 World's Fair.

I have written and rewritten other guidebooks (one of which, *The Funseeker's New Orleans,* was the last New Orleans guidebook published before Hurricane Katrina hit). Along the way, I have written a large number of magazine articles, a thesis (about Harry Hopkins, the W.P.A. head in the 1930s, and his time running the Red Cross in New Orleans in World War I), and a dissertation (on the nineteenth-century water infrastructure of New Orleans).

I have spent a lot of time at a keyboard. I have also spent a lot of time reading books. Reading, for me, can be a part of work: I have to do research for my writing and I teach history. That is not to say that nonfiction is boring. The good stuff is never boring.

I primarily like to read for pleasure. For New Orleans books, I can say that there is nothing that makes me laugh more than *A Confederacy of Dunces* by John Kennedy Toole. What a marvelous writer! And, of course, it is sad that he never knew of his success. But he is someone this city does treasure. There is the Ignatius Reilly statue on Canal Street where D. H. Holmes Co., Ltd., once stood. And there is a baby cup of his, donated by his mother to the Special Collections Division of the Tulane Library, with tiny teeth marks—a poignant souvenir of a grand talent.

I also enjoy the Louisiana novels of Frances Parkinson Keyes. I know they're "chick-lit," but, as you might say of that other local staple, Elmer's Gold Brick Eggs in my Easter basket: even if they are not good for me, I still like them.

I happily reread Barbara Hambly's series of detective novels set in nineteenth-century New Orleans and starring Benjamin January (or Janvier), free man of color. Shirley Ann Grau's *The House on Coli-*

seum Street and Sheila Bosworth's *Almost Innocent* are favorite novels of mine. And, for a sentimental children's book, I would pick Cecilia Jamison's *Lady Jane*. I think the script of Tennessee Williams's *A Streetcar Named Desire* contains perhaps the best use of words of anything ever written about this city.

I also still enjoy Walker Percy's *The Moviegoer*. (Read Williams's description of Elysian Fields Avenue, where Stella and Stanley live. Then, read the narrative about Binx Bolling's bus ride along that same route in Percy's book. Several decades separate those descriptions, but even over half a century later, Elysian Fields looks the same.)

New Orleans has great food writers and music writers and investigative reporter-writers. (Jason Berry's works concerning the Catholic Church are remarkable and important.)

The city has enough poets to regularly fill small collections, and you can hear them read their works at poetry slams and forums (try the Maple Leaf Bar on Maple Street). The late Maxine Cassin, a poet, was a friend, and I still remember the poem she wrote for the Steuben Glass Company about a vase: "Seven Pristine Gazelles."

New Orleans has a long tradition as a newspaper town. Today the *Times-Picayune* is still bringing out a paper, as it has under one name or another since 1837. There is a good weekly, *Gambit*. *New Orleans* magazine comes out monthly and there are academic and other literary publications.

Besides reading the work of its writers, New Orleans celebrates them. There is a Tennessee Williams Festival each spring, and the Pirate's Alley Faulkner Society sponsors the Words & Music Arts Festival and a writing contest. Faulkner House Books is one of several locally owned bookstores, as are the Garden District Book Shop and the Maple Street and Octavia Street bookstores.

Not only writers depict this city: filmmakers have used New Orleans as both a topic and as a backdrop for their stories. Elia Kazan's *Panic in the Streets* is a raw portrait of the 1950 underbelly of the French Quarter, not just another film noir. And, on any given day, there is a movie being planned or shooting in New Orleans. Thanks to some imaginative state tax laws, the film industry is omnipresent in this city.

New Orleans, after all, exists not only in reality, but in our personal

New Orleans of the mind that we all carry with us. It is the artists in words who generously give us that mental picture.

In this section I will acquaint you with some writers of the past, discuss a defunct newspaper, introduce you to a one-time editor and to a gossip columnist, showcase a cartoonist, touch on writers' addresses, explore how New Orleans got the nickname "the Big Easy," and remember a long ago bookstore. And I will share my memories of the *Times-Picayune*.

Frank Yerby and Marcus Christian

FRANK YERBY'S NOVELS always provide a good, page-turning story. The books may not be great works, but they are good reads. I grew up sneaking into the adult section of the public library, and these books were magnets for a teenaged reader. I knew nothing about Yerby himself, but knowing more about him makes him more interesting.

Marcus Christian was someone I came on when I seriously began work on New Orleans history. The library at the University of New Orleans has his papers (lots of them) and his work was wide ranging. He was part of the Federal Writers' Project of the Works Progress Administration in the 1930s, and he worked on the "American Slave Narratives" project, interviewing former slaves, asking a set series of questions. Marcus Christian was a good interviewer, and also a clear and knowledgeable writer.

Early nineteenth-century New Orleans provided a wealth of material for twentieth-century writers. One of the writers who made good use of the topic was Frank Yerby. Yerby's historical romances, which he called "costume" novels, were regulars on the best seller lists in the decades beginning with the 1940s. Yerby wrote of valiant heroes and beautiful heroines and used lush settings; none of his southern-based works were far from the norm for that genre. Besides, he was a good storyteller and was widely read. Yerby's uniqueness came from the fact that he was an African American.

Frank Yerby's first novel, *The Foxes of Harrow,* burst on the publishing world in 1946. It was an immediate hit. The book sold two million copies, was translated into twelve languages, and in 1951 was made into a movie starring Rex Harrison and Maureen O'Hara. The plot—or the tangle of interlocking plots—concerns a shrewd cardshark named Stephen Fox who becomes a sugar planter on the Mis-

Marcus Christian. Photo courtesy of Louisiana and Special Collections, Earl K. Long Library, University of New Orleans.

sissippi above New Orleans, marries into a local Creole family, has a New Orleans free woman of color as a mistress, and is a Confederate sympathizer in the Civil War. There is a fascinating character, a slave named Inch, who studies law in Paris, tries to escape north but is returned, and finally prospers during the occupation of New Orleans in the Civil War. The long family saga stretches over generations and takes in most of the relevant Louisiana history of the early-to-mid-nineteenth century.

Certainly the complicated lives of Orleanians of all races in the 1800s provided ample story lines. Yerby's choice of material, however, annoyed another African American writer, New Orleans resident Marcus Christian. Christian was apparently convinced that Yerby had stolen his story from material Christian himself had collected.

As recounted by poet and playwright Tom Dent in the spring 1984 issue of the quarterly *Black American Literature Forum*, Christian harbored resentment against Yerby, believing that *The Foxes of Harrow* plot came from the saga of a Houma family that Christian himself had discovered. When Dent was a teen-ager, he met Christian while working at the Dillard University library one summer. Dent's father, Albert W. Dent, was president of Dillard, and Christian was an assistant librarian regaling his fellow workers with readings of African American fables on his lunch hour. Christian had immersed himself in the history of New Orleans African Americans and had amassed a large collection of material, now housed at the University of New Orleans Earl K. Long Library.

Marcus Christian, born in 1900, had struggled on his own as a poet and writer. In the late Depression years he was headquartered at Dillard as director of the African American section of the New Orleans Federal Writers' Project. Christian also gathered the material that would be published in the 1970s as his *Negro Iron Workers of Louisiana: 1718–1900*. He completed a thousand pages of a manuscript on the history of African Americans in Louisiana, but it never became a book.

During Hurricane Betsy in 1965, Christian's Ninth Ward home was flooded, and as an added insult he was arrested as a looter when he tried to return home to salvage what he could of his collection.

In his last years, Marcus Christian was made a member of the history department at U.N.O. and was able to teach and tell his stories to young people, including Tom Dent, who remained a friend until Christian's death in 1976.

Marcus Christian's resentment of Frank Yerby never lessened over the years. Yerby himself was also capable of holding grudges. He was born in Augusta, Georgia, in 1916. His mother was a former teacher, and his father worked in Miami and Detroit as a hotel doorman. Yerby and his sister and two younger brothers attended Haines Institute, a local private grammar and high school for African Americans. Yerby, who was a good student and an avid reader, then attended and graduated from Paine College, an all-black Augusta institution where he began to write seriously.

Certainly growing up in the segregated South was difficult for a young African American. Yerby's family was of mixed race and most had light skin, and while the Yerby children in their private schools were sheltered from some harsh realities of racism, they could not escape it. Yerby graduated from Paine and then went to graduate school at Nashville's Fisk University, another African American college.

After he earned a master's degree, Yerby was accepted for doctoral studies in English at the University of Chicago. While the economic hardships of the Depression kept him from completing his degree, Yerby profited greatly from his Chicago years.

Just as Marcus Christian found kindred writers and interesting topics in the Federal Writers' Project, so did Yerby, whose acquaintances included African American writers Richard Wright and (Louisiana native) poet Arna Bontemps.

When Yerby left Chicago he taught for a year at Florida A & M University. Then, from 1939 to 1941, he taught in Baton Rouge at Southern University.

Yerby's time in Louisiana may not have been happy—in his obituary in the *Atlanta Constitution* he was quoted as saying that his employer, Southern University, was "an Uncle Tom factory." But it was at this point that he met Marcus Christian and learned the stories of Louisiana and the African Americans of the state that Christian was so proud of and eager to record.

Yerby's entrance onto the scene of American literature came with a short story in 1944, "The Health Card," about a black couple encountering prejudice in the military. He won the O. Henry Award. And then, in 1946, *The Foxes of Harrow* appeared and Yerby's fortune was made.

He had married and moved to New York with his family, where they apparently encountered prejudice—all of which was suddenly quelled when he began depositing his sizeable royalties in the local bank. But Yerby was soured on America. The family moved to France, but soon his wife returned home with her children and Yerby moved on to Spain. He married a Spanish woman, raised a family there, and regular as clockwork turned out best sellers for decades.

Yerby would continue to mine Louisiana for characters and plots in his "costume novels," even writing *The Girl from Storyville*, which built a story around the woman who posed as a supine nude in one of photographer Ernest J. Bellocq's best-known Storyville photos.

Although a few of his later works deal with black subjects, Yerby never considered himself a writer who took racial topics as his themes. His contribution to African American literature comes from his own existence, as an African American writer who found his own voice.

Marcus Christian may not have published as much as Yerby, but his intense devotion to his topic and his innate kindness in sharing his materials with others, coupled with his pride in his African American heritage, earn him a special place of honor in New Orleans literature.

Frances Parkinson Keyes and Crescent Carnival

When, as a teenager, I first met Estelle Lenoir Fontaine, Frances Parkinson Keyes's heroine in the 1945 novel *Crescent Carnival,* I thought she was the most romantic, saddest heroine I had ever known. On rereading the book, I decided she had no gumption at all and just needed a good dose of courage. Still later, I decided that Estelle was undoubtedly passive-aggressive, totally dysfunctional as a parent, and deserved everything she got.

Reading this book again is rather like visiting the home of old friends—you find the same flaws and the same good qualities, and if the flaws outweigh the good qualities this time, then there is still something comforting about being in familiar surroundings.

Estelle as a literary creation is no match for Scarlet O'Hara. Mrs. Keyes is no Margaret Mitchell, either, in many ways. But for all her lack of dimension, and her dislikeability, I am still Estelle's devoted friend. For all her faults, she is fascinating.

So, for that matter, is Mrs. Keyes. And, unlike Estelle, she had an adventurous life, filled with travel and hard intellectual work.

American women's magazines were where Mrs. Keyes earned her literary spurs. She was a long-time editor of *Good Housekeeping* and continued with occasional magazine pieces throughout her life. In fact, her ancestral home in Newbury, Vermont, was not even very far from the home of that greatest of early magazine writers, Sarah Josepha Hale.

Mrs. Keyes gravitated to the richness and regularity of patterned society. Perhaps this contributed to her decision to convert to Roman Catholicism in 1939. For whatever reason, she was drawn to the symbolism of Carnival season in New Orleans and immediately chose it as her theme when she had decided to move here to write a book.

The Beauregard-Keyes House museum, 1113 Chartres Street. Photo by Carolyn Kolb.

Mrs. Keyes, in her own way, used her fiction to spread information about our city and state, and she tried very hard to be accurate. That other writers had more heart is none of her doing—but she was a cracking good storyteller.

New Orleans, as Mrs. Keyes learned, is a place of contrasts and conflict—that's what makes it such a good literary topic. The New Orleans of the 1940s in which Mrs. Keyes wrote this book was in many ways different from the city today. It may have had more people, but somehow it seemed smaller, more closely knit. And here comes Mrs. Keyes, already a best-selling author, moving to town as a total stranger, specifically to write a novel. She would stay in the state for part of each year until she died thirty years, and several novels, later.

It is tempting to think that Mrs. Keyes took a look at *Gone with the Wind* and decided she could do that: multipaged southern saga, heavy on romance, make a great movie. It is also possible that part of her reasoning had to do with the war in Europe: she liked living and writing books in exotic locations, and New Orleans was about as exotic as you could get without leaving the country.

The plot of *Crescent Carnival* concerns star-crossed lovers in three generations of two New Orleans families. In 1890, Estelle Lenoir is a Creole, and lives in the French Quarter. She falls in love with Andrew "Andy" Breckenridge, an American widower who lives in the Garden District. Her parents forbid them to marry, she is not courageous enough to defy them, and Estelle is forced to marry another Creole. Andy dies in a steamboat wreck after marrying Estelle's husband's sister.

In 1913, the by-now widowed Estelle's daughter, Marie Celeste Fontaine, falls in love with Breckenridge's son by his first marriage, Breck, Junior, who is, by this time, already married. Breck drowns, Marie Celeste runs to a convent and joins the Carmelites. Finally, by the late 1930s, Estelle thinks she will get her granddaughter Stella Fontaine together with the Breckenridge grandson, Drew the third—when that fails miserably, Estelle settles for seeing that Drew is united with the right woman for him, Patty Forrestal (who is actually a distant cousin). As the *Times-Picayune* reviewer pointed out, when Patty Forrestal and Drew Breckenridge decide to call Andrew Breckenridge the fourth Ken they "complete all the interesting variations of that over used name."

The reviewer then closed by saying: "This is lusty melodrama of the escape fiction class. It is a rather satisfying book. Little is left to the imagination and all the ends are neatly tied."

It says something of the literary muscle of Mrs. Keyes that the book was already out in November of 1942—the last scenes in the novel take place just after Pearl Harbor, in December of 1941, and her preface mentions that she was writing in New Orleans up until August of 1942. To get an eight-hundred-page novel finished and through production and printing and into the stores in mere months is phenomenal—and there was a war on!

Crescent Carnival is long and incredibly inclusive. The characters have a tendency to spout off facts like a guidebook, or an encyclopedia article. Mrs. Keyes also put in letters, or newspaper clippings (some of them actual news stories, with a fictional character thrown in). She includes the entire floor plan for a plantation house and when she describes her characters' homes she has specific houses in mind.

Keyes invents from whole cloth a Carnival krewe, the Pacifici—presumably naming them in a little salute to Atlanteans. She has numerous song lyrics, some in French. She tucks in anecdotes, puts occasional real people in as minor characters. She has set pieces: a quail hunt, a dinner with an operatic troop, a visit to a small shrine, a description of a flood, marine recruiting in southwest Louisiana, the Metropolitan Opera's annual visit to New Orleans. She includes full treatments on the mechanics of a Carnival ball, the turn of the century Louisiana lottery, the death of Huey Long, the reform movement of Progressivism. This is a giant municipal landfill of a novel—there is a little bit of everything thrown in, in helter-skelter order.

Crescent Carnival is an odd blend of fiction and nonfiction, but then so are many other best sellers. Mrs. Keyes's characters are one-dimensional; each could be described more as a type than as a person. But her types are so universal that her characters sometimes resemble real individuals.

Perhaps the best way to categorize Mrs. Keyes and her novel are to think of her as a wandering minstrel traveling to a castle and making up a song from the local stories she hears. She listens to the stories people tell her; then she is the one who makes them into a song, and she takes the song down the road to the next castle. The song is now hers. But the stories behind the song still belong, in a way, to the first people who told them to her. While it is very flattering to have someone want to listen to your story, it can also be a little annoying when they make it into their song and take it away.

Mrs. Keyes did indeed come to New Orleans and listen to stories. She sought out storytellers. She steeped herself in local facts. She was an outsider and could claim no personal ownership of these stories, but she was the one who would put them together into a text, into which she also wove a great deal of herself. She freely acknowledged her debt to those who helped: in the first line of her preface she notes, "Never have I written a book for which I felt the credit was so little due to myself."

Mrs. Keyes's treating of race relations is based right in her time period, subtly but not overtly racist. She deals with African American characters on two levels. She puts in a number of folk tales and anecdotes and vignettes of real characters as cooks and housekeepers, and she credits some of her white informants with supplying her with stories. On another level, she creates fictional characters and has a mixed

Frances Parkinson Keyes's desk, the Beauregard-Keyes House museum, 1113 Chartres Street. Photo by Carolyn Kolb.

race family group shadowing Estelle Lenoir and the Fontaines—one of the Fontaines in the past had a liaison with a free woman of color and the connection is repeated in the next generation.

Whatever Mrs. Keyes's own views on race, her original typed manuscript of *Crescent Carnival* is held in the library of New Orleans's Xavier University, the preeminent Catholic African American university in the country. The manuscript was part of a prize in a war bond–selling contest for college libraries during World War II. The "Treasury Department War Bond Literary Collection" also includes works by Adam Clayton Powell, Langston Hughes, and Mark Van Doren.

A Keyes book is a good read, and, if you choose the right one, it gives you a good short course in basic Louisiana history. While *Blue Camellia* told the story of the Louisiana rice industry and was written while Mrs. Keyes was living near Crowley, *The River Road* was about the Louisiana sugar industry and was written while she lived at The

Cottage Plantation on the Mississippi River near Baton Rouge. So, when I was working on a story about Louisiana sugar families I reread *The River Road* before I drove to my first interview, at a house not far from where Keyes had lived while writing the book.

While I sat chatting with my interviewee, a retired longtime sugar planter, and his wife, I questioned whether *The River Road* might have some basis in anecdotes or facts about the area. What did I mean, my subject asked? "Well," I said, "did you ever hear of anyone passing out in a cane truck and getting pulled into the grinder?" At that point his wife commented that she hadn't been able to forget that gruesome detail, either.

Apparently Mrs. Keyes's readers must include mainly females and few sugar planters. "Who would put something that awful in a book?" he asked. "Who would want to read that?" He looked accusingly at the only two females present. It was not a good moment for Keyes fans.

Keyes's books, while no longer big sellers, do have some staying power. Her very first novel, *The Old Gray Homestead*, is part of Project Gutenberg and is available online for free. Her *Mother Cabrini: Missionary to the World* is in print—and recommended on websites for Catholics who homeschool their children. Also, her novel *Joy Street*, set in Boston, was republished in 1997.

And, I am happy to report, *Crescent Carnival* or, in its alternate title *If Ever I Cease to Love*, is still readily available used from amazon.com, and, no doubt, copies may be gathering dust on shelves in Louisiana stores that sell used books.

Romantic New Orleans somehow never really goes out of fashion.

The New Orleans Item

DURING THE NINETEENTH and early twentieth centuries New Orleans was a big newspaper town—there is even a section of Camp Street between Lafayette Square and Poydras that used to be called newspaper row for the number of papers published there. Somehow all those different papers evolved into the one daily paper serving the city today. The *Times-Picayune* (denoting two original newspapers, the *Times* and *Picayune,*) until recently was also formerly known as the *Times-Picayune States-Item,* with the *States-Item* (two more names) as the *Picayune*'s afternoon paper.

Prior to 1958, the *Times-Picayune* published an afternoon paper called the *States,* in competition with another locally owned paper, the *New Orleans Item.*

In June 1952, the *New Orleans Item* celebrated its seventy-fifth year of publication with a commemorative issue, full of facts about the paper's history. It began in 1877 as a cooperative venture by twelve printers, who bought the press of the suddenly defunct daily, the *Republican,* which folded for lack of readership when Reconstruction ended, U.S. Army troops withdrew, and a Democrat, Francis T. Nicholls, was elected governor. The *Daily City Item* would be the first evening daily newspaper published in the South. The older papers in town (including the *Times* and the *Picayune*) had national news contacts. The *Item* would focus on local stories.

In days when newspapers were the only place to get the news, there was tough competition for stories. Reporters would dash back just in time for their final editions. The morning paper reporters had the luxury of working till midnight or so, but the evening reporters started their days at dawn, struggling to get fresh news onto the pages that folks bought to read riding on the streetcar home from work. There would be editions, coming from one paper or another,

75th Anniversary Edition

NEW ORLEANS ITEM

FINAL HOME

To Our Readers

Truman Asks Steel Seizure

Issue Put Before Congress

31 Red PWs, One GI Killed In Koje Island Crackdown

N. O. 1-Package Bill Is Given New Hope

Clear U. S. In Texas City Blast

Ingrid Gets Assist From Film Chief

Take Along Umbrella To Keep Dry

Bulletins

Told To Wear Panties And Fringes

Bourbon Dancers Confused

Item Index

WDSU-NBC

The seventy-fifth anniversary edition of the *New Orleans Item*. Used with permission of the *Times-Picayune*.

around the clock. There was home delivery, but sales from newsstands and, especially for afternoon papers, from street vendors was brisk and competitive. Just as today, reporters had personalities and quirks, and columnists could build followings all their own.

The *Item* had a real presence in New Orleans, and it had a specific, and opinionated, voice and hard-driving reporters. Hermann Deutsch, who would later shift his column to a *Picayune*-owned paper, was a prominent *Item* reporter, as was *Item* associate editor Bill Monroe—who would later spend time at WDSU-TV and with NBC-TV as a longtime news personality. The *Item*'s 1952 board of directors included such prominent Orleanians as John Minor Wisdom (later a federal judge), Herman Kohlmeyer, Monte Lemann, and Edgar A. G. Bright.

The *Item,* although it was never financially strong, was always politically active, and on the liberal end of the spectrum. In 1920, for example, the *Item* championed the fight to make Louisiana the thirty-sixth state to ratify the constitutional amendment giving women the right to vote (that effort failed: Tennessee would be the thirty-sixth state to ratify). During the Long era, the *Item* could be counted on to be against Huey—with the exception that the *Item* prophetically came out in favor of Long's idea to stop cotton production one Depression year so the price of the crop would rise the next year. That plan failed, but the concept of government-sponsored crop reduction would be a part of American farm policy for decades.

The *Item* was purchased in 1949 by a group headed by David Stern III, a Harvard graduate born in Philadelphia and raised in New Jersey. Stern—a former World War II army captain who was perhaps better known as the author of "Francis, the Famous Talking Mule" from which a string of B-movies were made—continued the *Item*'s tradition of reformist policy and gave its editorial page a decidedly liberal cast. In 1954, when the sewerage and water board was considering whether or not to add fluoride to New Orleans water, Stern, supporting the addition of fluoride for tooth decay prevention, pointed out in an editorial that bad teeth "caused 21 per cent of the rejections among the first two million young men called for the draft in World War II." (The editorial did no good: New Orleanians had no fluoridation until the 1970s.)

In one of the *Item*'s most popular actions, the newspaper led a drive to secure an elephant for the Audubon Zoo. Schoolchildren of the city contributed pennies and nickels, and an African elephant, female, was purchased in 1924. A contest was held to select a name for the new zoo resident, and Itema was chosen, and until her death years later she was a popular zoo attraction.

New Orleans television owed much to the *Item*—two alumni were Phil Johnson, long-time editorialist and news director at WWL-TV, and WWL-TV sportscaster Hap Glaudi. Glaudi's column in the *Item* was titled "Looking 'Em Over" and was a must-read for fans of everything from fishing to baseball. However, the *Item*'s competitors were not just after crime news or sports stories—even the society section had scoops and rivalry.

One *Picayune* society reporter remembered that "we all used to try to have the first engagement announcement—we wanted to know it when only the family knew it." Once a new young *Item* female reporter/photographer spotted two young ladies at the intermission of a play. "May I take your picture for the *Item*?" she asked. The young ladies started to comply, but honesty won out and they had to confess that no, she couldn't—they both worked for the *Times-Picayune*.

If there were differences between the two papers, it would be that the *Item* was more liberal and more flamboyant, with juicier headlines, and the *Picayune* and *States* were a little more conservative and staid.

The *Item* differed from the *Times-Picayune* in another way—the *Item* had unions, and the *Picayune* never did. The press unions actually took out a congratulatory ad in the *Item*'s 1952 anniversary edition.

Although the realities of trying to compete with a well-financed opponent finally brought the *Item* to the point of sale to the *Picayune* company in 1958, many of its reporters and staff continued to make a mark on the city, and on its news.

The legacy of the *Item* extended to literature. Harnett Kane, author of numerous books on Louisiana and southern history, spent thirteen years on the *Item* news desk. Hamilton Basso, once a popular novelist, claimed an *Item* heritage. Carl Carmer wrote the classic *Stars Fell on Alabama* after serving on the *Item*. Harold Ross, the quintessential American magazine editor, was once an *Item* staffer before the *New Yorker* claimed him. And Albert Goldstein, once a director of the *Double Dealer*—New Orleans 1920s-era literary magazine—was one *Item* veteran who later went to the *Picayune*.

One *Item* memento could be termed bizarre. I was once at a dinner party in a dining room with lovely cypress paneling on the walls. "Where did you get that paneling?" we all asked the host. "Oh, it's from an old building," he said. When pressed, he explained. "Actually, these were the swinging doors from the men's room at the *Item*." You could guess that even the lowliest part of the building was still in a position to collect some gossipy stories.

Roark Bradford

Any discussion of the good old days of New Orleans journalism would have to bring in the name of Roark Bradford. In the French Quarter of the 1920s he provided a measure of literary excitement in the city, and he and his wife, Mary Rose, were known as fun-loving party-givers extraordinaire.

Oddly enough, Bradford will be forever associated with Christmas: first, for a character of that name he helped invent, and second, for a brief piece of fiction published just after his death and purporting to relate the true story of that annual holiday.

He was born Roark Whitney Wickliffe Bradford in 1896 in Lauderdale County, Tennessee. He served in the army reserve in World War I, spent some time as a student at the University of California, and began work as a journalist for a series of southern newspapers, including the *Lafayette Daily Advertiser* in 1923. In 1924 he came to New Orleans to work for the *Times-Picayune* as the night side city editor, and he soon was promoted to Sunday editor.

Literary life in the 1920s French Quarter was active and fun. Prolific nonfiction writer Lyle Saxon had moved to the Quarter some years before, and was leader of a group of writers and journalists who kept things amusing. There was the literary magazine the *Double Dealer*, there were local daily papers (besides the *Picayune*, there were *the New Orleans States* and the *New Orleans Item*), and there was a constant stream of literary figures moving in and out of town. Sherwood Anderson, midwestern author of the scandalous collection *Winesburg, Ohio*, was ensconced in an apartment in the lower Pontalba apartments on Jackson Square. Young poet William Faulkner came down from Oxford, Mississippi, to laze in the Quarter's heady atmosphere.

Bradford, a widower, had married Mary Rose Sciarra Himler. The Bradfords lived in a Creole cottage at 719 Toulouse Street (where

Roark Bradford. Photo courtesy of Louisiana Division/City Archives, New Orleans Public Library.

Wehmeier's Belt Shop was most recently located) and were known for their legendary parties. Did Gertrude Stein and Alice B. Toklas sit silent on a sofa for an entire evening until they left? Perhaps. If so, they were among the few who ever kept quiet in the Bradford ménage. Supposedly a skeleton was found buried in the patio, but at the behest of the Bradfords this event was hushed up, too.

Bradford as Sunday editor of the *Picayune* had discretion in buying freelance work, thus helping young writers. It is said that William Faulkner received his first check for a piece of fiction from Bradford for one of Faulkner's *New Orleans Sketches,* later collected in book form.

Like other New Orleans journalists, Bradford was well aware of the legends and lore of the city. And, like his pal Lyle Saxon, Bradford could get peeved at the moonlight and magnolias memories that were so popular with outsiders. One especially liquid evening of enjoyment found Saxon and Bradford with great glee creating, out of their fertile imaginations, a brand-new New Orleans legend. Thus, that fierce, tall riverboat woman Annie Christmas was born—she could outfight anything, man, bear, or alligator, had flaming red hair and a temper to match. Actually, she would have been named "Mary Christmas," but Mary Rose pointed out that was a bit much, so "Annie" she became. Her exploits, tongue firmly in cheek, made it into print. Strangely enough, Annie Christmas began appearing in other writers' works, and was soon enshrined in the pantheon of New Orleans figures—even in recent years when the city sported actors in character playing familiar New Orleans personalities on French Quarter streets during the holidays, Annie Christmas was proudly in that number.

Like many another newspaper editor, Roark Bradford longed to write fiction. So, in 1926, he quit his day job and started to write. The next year he won an O. Henry Award for his short story "Child of God." Bradford was a prolific writer, turning out short stories, short plays, books, musicals, and he even had one work become a major film. But he is little read today. The reason? Roark Bradford wrote in dialect, an approximation of what he thought was typical African American speech. Critics today point to his characters and his writing and brand his work racist. The critics are correct.

And yet, there is something about Bradford's work that carries simple, moral truths, that tells a good story, that is sympathetic. Bradford supposedly liked to write in the country, using a kerosene lamp, so he could get the flavor of the world he was creating. It is a simple world, where preachers and Bible stories mix easily in everyday life. One collection of his stories, *Ol' Man Adam an' His Chillun,* concerned an African American preacher explaining the Old Testament to his congregation in terms they understood. Heaven, they learned, was a place with a bayou, and there was a fish fry every day and good cigars to smoke. The book was transformed by playwright Marc Connelly into the play *The Green Pastures,* and won a Pulitzer Prize in 1930. In 1936, it was made into the first major movie with an all-black cast. In spite of its fanciful storyline, even the *New York Times* current online movie review notes that it is well acted, and has "a lot more clarity, profundity and spiritual reverence than most 'serious' Biblical adaptations."

Bradford did not limit his writing to dialect stories, but he did work with other types of folktales. His book on the folk hero John Henry, not written in dialect, was made into a musical and told the story of the legendary steel-driving man whose great heart led him to try to defeat a machine.

Bradford published some one hundred stories in *Collier's* magazine. In the December 24, 1948, issue his work "How Come Christmas" appeared. Again written in dialect, the story centers on a preacher, this time explaining to a group of children the significance of Christmas. The children, predictably, can't figure out who came first, Santa or Baby Jesus. And why is Christmas in winter and the Fourth of July in summer? As the story unfolds, George Washington defeats a king on the Fourth of July, and by Christmastime Baby Jesus prefers Santa's kind cradle gift of a shiny apple to gold and diamonds, and the Lord "passes a miracle" so Santa can make other children happy with gifts every year on Jesus's birthday. It's a kindly little tale that certainly puts things in moral perspective and keeps a little bit of the miraculous.

Bradford would die soon after its publication.

Mary Rose and their son, Richard, born in 1932, moved to Santa Fe, New Mexico. Richard wrote a poignant novel, *Red Sky at Morning*, about growing up there without his father. One of the themes of the book, set as it was in multiracial Santa Fe, was a harsh judgment of southern racism, amply disguised and expressed with good humor and sympathy. Had he had the opportunity to read his son's book, Roark might have understood a little better why his own work is less appreciated today.

Jill Jackson

JILL JACKSON was a New Orleans native who began her career here and was the first female sportscaster in America. She was still a Hollywood gossip columnist into her nineties, and she boasted a namesake salad on the menu at Brennan's—you just can't get much more famous than that!

On New Orleans airwaves in the mid-twentieth century, this blonde with a pageboy hairdo was a top local media personality. And everybody who rode a bus or streetcar read her entertainment column in *Rider's Digest,* a pamphlet produced for transit riders by New Orleans Public Service, Inc. She was a New Orleans girl, graduate of Sophie Wright High School and Newcomb College, and, when she permanently relocated to Hollywood nearly fifty years before she died, she left a local legacy.

Her memoirs have been published online at the Newcomb Center for Research on Women website (tulane.edu/nccrow/upload/jill jacksonmemoir.pdf). The title comes from a quip by an old out-of-work vaudeville performer who had taken a job tidying up after the elephants in a circus, and, when a friend urged giving up the undignified occupation, had exclaimed, "Whaaattt! And leave show business!!!" In the book, Jill Jackson's breezy attitude (and a memory of performing similar chores after an elephant appeared on her WWL-TV show) comes through in a series of snappy anecdotes about her media adventures in New Orleans from the 1940s to the 1960s and her life as an entertainment columnist in California after that.

Jill Jackson always made for good copy. "I'm still not a feminist," she insisted, after confirming the difficulties male sports reporters made for her (forcing her to sit outside the press box at football games in the rain, not providing convenient ladies' rooms). Was it miserable? "Don't be silly. I was having a ball. I loved every minute of it!"

Jill Jackson. Photo courtesy of Nadine Vorhoff Library, Newcomb Center for Research on Women, Tulane University.

In her book she mentions with gratitude those who helped her career along, one of whom was the late Mildred Fossier. Fossier, a friend from Newcomb, recalled their both acting in the dramatic club in college, and then at Le Petit Theatre du Vieux Carré. While there, the two young actresses "got into a lot of mischief," Fossier remembered. Once they started a rumor that Hollywood producer Darryl F. Zanuck was planning to attend a rehearsal. Then, they gleefully watched the resulting havoc. Jill Jackson "was a good actress . . . her sense of timing was pure comedy," Fossier said.

While at the theater, Jackson became friends with Peggy and Henry Dupré, and an invitation to be on Peggy Dupré's WWL radio show sparked a love for the medium, while her experience writing for the *New Orleans Item* newspaper provided a skill in reporting.

Jill Jackson was an accomplished athlete, a golf and tennis champion. Injuries unhappily put her on the sidelines. Her interests in sports and radio soon would coincide, as she explained in her memoirs: "Henry Dupré, of WWL, said, 'Help me cover the Louisiana State

Women's Golf Tournament.' I did. Richard Jones of Jax Beer heard me and asked, 'Would you like to try a five-day-a-week, five-minute sportscast?' I would, and I did on WSMB for seven years and it made history."

The Jax sponsorship also resulted in her taking up the professional name Jill Jackson, which she kept even though that sports show had ended by 1950. She would continue with her sports reporting career on WWL.

Jackson was resourceful in getting her stories. Women were barred from Tulane's football practices, so she observed from a nearby oak tree. The Quarterback Club luncheons were also closed to women. But since the events were held at the St. Charles Hotel (where Jackson was a resident, living in the suite that had once belonged to writer Lyle Saxon), the waiters were glad to pass on the gossip.

"For a shiny fifty-cent piece (remember when this was), they told me everything that went on inside," Jackson's memoir noted.

Jill Jackson covered everything from races at the fairgrounds (once running into difficulty because she was broadcasting predictions of winners) to deep-sea fishing (with a sprightly account of an uncomfortable stay at the Oleander Hotel on Grande Isle) to baseball (while on air with Dizzy Dean she dropped her purse and Dizzy regaled the audience by describing the contents).

Jackson's stock-in-trade was her humor. She always closed her Jax Beer sports show with a rhyme appropriate to that day's topic, once ending a hunting story with "I know a duck who seldom quacks. But, when he does, he says Jax, Jax, Jax."

Jackson was ultimately elected a member of the Associated Press Sportscasters' Club, and was made a member of *Esquire* magazine's sports poll (where her membership card was made out to MR. Jill Jackson). She was also a union member, at one time being in the American Federation of Television and Radio Artists, Actor's Equity, and the American Guild of Variety Artists—and that one came about because of her off-site broadcasting.

Jill Jackson left the studio for a weekly stint with a radio show from Brennan's Restaurant. Owner Owen Brennan was a good friend and a skilled promoter of his business, at that time located on Bourbon Street. Jackson's program showcased celebrities dining there.

A popular novel of the 1950s was *Dinner at Antoine's* by Frances Parkinson Keyes. One character in the novel was a blonde radio personality. "My mother thought that was me," Jackson admitted. The novel had one lasting effect in that the title inspired Owen Brennan to feature "Breakfast at Brennan's."

Jackson's namesake salad at Brennan's is described as "iceberg lettuce, chopped hard boiled egg, crumbled bacon, blue cheese, chives and Jackson dressing."

Jackson moved to WWL-TV with her own interview show. She had switched from sports to entertainment coverage, and seemed to have met every movie star and actor who visited the city. This led Charles "Pie" Dufour to suggest that she write an entertainment column for the *Rider's Digest*.

Her celebrity acquaintances, and her regular visits to California, finally led to a move to that state. She even appeared in some films, including *Airport*. For eighteen years her column appeared in the *Times-Picayune*. Her only other local outlet was the *Driftwood* of the University of New Orleans, while the late Don Lee Keith was teaching journalism there.

Jill Jackson was working on her autobiography when she spoke with Beth Willinger, now a research professor at the Newcomb College Center for Research on Women. Online publication seemed appropriate. "I was most attracted to the story because she was the first female sportscaster in the United States, as far as we can tell. Also, she was right at this bridge over radio and television in New Orleans, an interesting time historically," Willinger said.

When I interviewed her for this article in 2008, Jill Jackson was still turning out eight hundred or nine hundred words a week on her faithful Olivetti typewriter ("I'm a technophobe," she admitted). She may not have visited the city in years, but that did not mean she didn't still have an interest in what goes on here. She got right to the point: "So, are Brad and Angelina going to sell that house in the French Quarter?"

These days who will tell us such things? Obviously, Jill Jackson is missed.

John Chase

PATRONS CHECKING OUT BOOKS at the main branch of the New Orleans Public Library need never be bored. There, on the wall in front of them, stretches a giant mural, sixty-three feet long and ten feet high, a cartoon map of Louisiana with illustrations telling the history of the area, the culture of the region, the products and the wildlife and, indeed, the story of the state. The mural was a gift of the students and teachers at Dillard University. The lines of the mural are simple but the design work is deft and clever. There's obviously a little genius behind this art work—and his name was John Churchill Chase.

September 17, 2005, was the hundredth anniversary of John Chase's birth. A native of the city who unashamedly loved New Orleans, he was an artist whose medium of choice was the cartoon, and we were fortunate to have him as a resource until his death in 1986.

Most remarkably, John Chase was an editorial cartoonist on television—most likely the first and only one—and prior to that, his editorial cartoons were seen in the daily paper. His alter ego, or at least his signature character, was a short male with glasses, a moustache, and a small hat. "Mr. Taxpayer" or "The Little Man" seemed to meet life's crises with both surprise and resilience, whether it was a politician in eighteenth-century French court dress labeled "King Hooey XIV" (as Chase christened Huey Long) or a giant bag of money titled "Billion Dollar Cost of One Hurricane."

John Chase was born in New Orleans, the first child of Natalie Octavia Neelis and Joseph Carter Chase. A brother, Francis, and a sister, Susanna, would complete the family. His father died when John Chase was ten. His mother took her young family to live with her brother in Gueydan, Louisiana, but when the family returned to New

John Chase's mural at the New Orleans Public Library. Photo by Carolyn Kolb.

Orleans, Chase attended Isidore Newman School, where he met a lifelong friend, writer and historian Charles L. "Pie" Dufour.

In an interview in the 1969 book of his cartoons, *Of Time and Chase*, edited by Edison B. Allen, Chase admitted that "all I ever wanted to be was a cartoonist." After high school, he enrolled at the Chicago Academy of Fine Arts, where "I learned then that to be a cartoonist you first had to learn to draw." Chase was left-handed, but, as he reminded his teachers, so was Leonardo da Vinci.

After art school, he became an assistant to cartoonist Frank King, who drew the comic strip *Gasoline Alley* in Chicago. Soon, he returned to New Orleans and in 1925 became the editorial cartoonist for the *Morning Tribune*, a short-lived venture of the afternoon *Item*.

In 1934, Chase married Frances Nicholson, whom he met when she visited the *Item* promoting circulation contests. The couple would have three children: Cathryn, Frances, and John Chase, Jr.

Chase, along with his friend, reporter Hermann Deutsch, covered the assassination of Huey Long for the *Item*. Since photographers were barred, Chase's quick drawings were the only illustrations available and were reprinted nationwide.

In 1947, Chase switched to the *New Orleans States,* and besides continuing his editorial cartoons, fostered his growing interest in New Orleans history. He illustrated a centennial history of the D. H. Holmes department store; he illustrated volumes of popular history from writer Robert Tallant and his friends Deutsch and Dufour. He joined the Toastmasters organization and began making talks. One such talk on the history of New Orleans through its street names led to his still-popular book, *Frenchmen, Desire, Good Children,* first published in 1949.

Chase's surviving child, Frances Chase Shelton, remembers that her father liked going to Sunday Mass at St. Louis Cathedral. "We would take a long, meandering way home. He liked to go to different neighborhoods, ride around looking at different parts of the city," she recalled. "Obviously, he was researching his book." Her mother typed the manuscript three times, she added.

As an additional history project, for the sesquicentennial of the Louisiana Purchase in 1953, Chase produced a series of cartoons that ran in newspapers across the country, and this later became a school textbook.

One of her father's activities Frances Shelton particularly remembered was his work on football game covers. "He worked all summer on them, all the universities must have had the same deadlines." Chase would eventually draw covers for L.S.U., Tulane, Rice, the University of Texas, Georgia Tech, the University of Kentucky, the University of Alabama, the University of Florida, and Virginia Tech. Professional football teams he drew covers for included the Kansas City Chiefs, the Dallas Texans, and the Houston Oilers.

In 1967 Chase made a remarkable career change: he became the editorial cartoonist for WDSU-TV.

"He did not seek me out, I sought him out," explained John Corporon, then WDSU news editor and who, when interviewed about Chase in 2005, was retired and living in Brooklyn, New York. "I approached him and said, 'There has never been a cartoonist on television before,' and 'How would you like to be the first in the country?'"

Luckily for New Orleans, Chase took up the challenge. His evening cartoon would sometimes be complete except for a flourish and signature, added by that skilled left hand. Sometimes there would be more than one panel, and eventually the cartoons were in color.

As Corporon explained: "John and I would get our heads together five days a week between 9 and 10 in the morning. He would come up with ideas for possible cartoons, and if I had an opinion I might give him that view. But it was always his choice. We did collaborate a lot, but John was the driving force."

Chase was a resounding success. "I never got a single complaint from management on his cartoons and they rarely saw them in advance," Corporon marveled.

In the 1970s, John Chase took on an artistic challenge from St. Dominic's Catholic Church, on Harrison Avenue near Canal Boulevard.

"We still had the large window to complete," according to Father Victor Brown, then pastor of St. Dominic's and who, in 2005, was in Lufkin, Texas, at a Dominican monastery. "We were having a meeting of the parish council and talking about it, and finding an artist, and someone suggested, 'Why not give John Chase a chance to create something?' and I said, 'Well, he's a cartoonist.'"

Father Brown recalled, "My first thought was 'Oh, he'll draw our Lord with a funny hat and a little mustache.' But I did call him, and I explained that we hoped he might design something for us. And first he said, 'In stained glass? I've never done anything in stained glass.' But he said he would try."

The giant stained glass window portrays "The Transfiguration," with Jesus between Moses and Elijah. "It shows our Lord, very young and without a beard," Father Brown described. "It's a glorious window, and he was very proud of it."

Frances Chase Shelton noted, "As my father grew older through the years, his 'Mr. Taxpayer' grew older, too." One fond memory she treasures involved his effect on his readers. "I had taken a cab to my father's funeral, and when I told the taxi driver where I was going, he said, 'John Chase? I didn't know him but I sure looked at his cartoons.'"

That was John Chase's true talent. His work spoke directly to his readers.

2900 Prytania Street

IN A CITY LIKE NEW ORLEANS it shouldn't seem strange that you might find yourself living in what was once the home of a famous writer. I am fortunate: that has happened to me twice.

My husband and I had an apartment at 431 Royal Street in the French Quarter—right next door to Brennan's Restaurant. (Brennan's was a great neighbor. One Thanksgiving they filled up a casserole for me with oyster dressing: mine was a dismal, salty failure.) But 431 Royal was also the place where Tennessee Williams rented a room on an early New Orleans visit.

My first apartment after college was upstairs at 2900 Prytania Street. And one of the former tenants there was a writer: F. Scott Fitzgerald.

Fitzgerald, the madcap master storyteller of the Jazz Age, was exactly the sort of person New Orleanians would like. Apparently, he felt a little something for New Orleans, too, because he spent some weeks here in early 1920.

A dropout from the class of 1917 at Princeton, Fitzgerald had joined the army and, stationed in Montgomery, Alabama, met a local belle, Zelda Sayre, and was smitten with her. She broke off their engagement in the summer of 1919 and he went home to St. Paul, Minnesota, to write. Over that fall, he began to be published. His first novel, *This Side of Paradise*, was accepted and was due out in the spring of 1920.

That winter of 1919–1920, Fitzgerald determined to go south to New Orleans. Several possible reasons for this have been suggested. His main biographer, Matthew Bruccoli, Ph.D., of the University of South Carolina, suggested that Fitzgerald was afraid of contracting tuberculosis during wintertime in frigid St. Paul. There is another little story that he decided that Zelda thought he wasn't "southern"

2900 Prytania Street. Photo by Carolyn Kolb.

enough, so he was trying to absorb something of the culture, even if New Orleans is not your typical southern city.

Is it possible he had met a school chum at Princeton who called New Orleans home and he was intrigued by the stories he had heard? Or, could it be that, with a novel due out in a few months, he cadged some extra money from his publisher for correcting proofs and gave himself a little vacation? He might also have picked a city close to Zelda, and one he thought might appeal to her, so that she might visit him there, away from her parents. She never did.

For whatever reason, Fitzgerald came to New Orleans, and from the return address he listed on telegrams and letters posted here, he lived at 2900 Prytania Street, beginning in January, for just a few weeks. We don't even know if he stayed for Carnival, on February 17 that year, with Elinor Bright (Richardson) reigning as queen. He mentions Mardi Gras in one short story, "The Jellybean," about a socially inept misfit, the sort of person who would let another fellow "take his girl to Mardi Gras." Bruccoli thinks his story "The Camel's Back" may have been written here.

The house at 2900 Prytania probably looks today very much like the house Fitzgerald knew (except that in yellow and green it is cheerier—it was probably all white in the 1920s). On the uptown river corner of Sixth and Prytania, it is a simple two-story wooden Greek Revival–style structure. In different configurations it has had varying numbers of apartments, has also been a single-family home, and is probably pre–Civil War.

The house at 2900 Prytania has other literary ties besides that of Fitzgerald. Catherine Koppel recalled that her father, the late Harwood "Woody" Koppel, had bought the house in 1974, but was using it as rental property until the 1980s when, at the children's urging, the Koppels moved in. "I had my last two years of high school there, my sister Ann (now an attorney) had all her high school years and my sister Mary (now an Episcopal priest) was beginning seventh grade." Their brother, also Woody, and, like his father, in real estate, was already in college when the children and their mother, Lyn, and father moved in.

The elder Woody Koppel was the one who spread the Fitzgerald story. Woody, besides serving on the Orleans Parish School Board, was an avid reader, as is Lyn. In fact, besides the Fitzgerald connection, Woody Koppel added a poet to the 2900 Prytania roster.

Everette Maddox, who wrote and taught here in the 1970s and 1980s, was known for his poetry sessions at the Maple Leaf Bar, published several collections of verse, and still has a following, decades after his death. Maddox was a resident, and he also wrote a poem entitled "2900 Prytania" and dedicated it "To Harwood Koppel." Maddox sings of "the wrought-iron balcony of a poem shaped just like my new 120-year old house," which he further describes as "a wooden lime peel hanging out of a lightning-murdered tree."

Poet Maxine Cassin thought that Maddox may have liked the Fitzgerald association of his address. Was Maddox like Fitzgerald? "Well, he did wear Brooks Brothers suits," Cassin admitted. Since one of his poetry collections was titled *Bar Scotch*, Maddox may have had another kinship with the hard-drinking Fitzgerald.

Catherine Koppel also pointed out that the Vampire Lestat had an address at Prytania and Sixth in one of Anne Rice's works. Since Prytania and Sixth is also across the street from the Lafayette Number 1 Cemetery, Lestat would have felt right at home.

When I lived in the upper front apartment at 2900 Prytania I had just graduated from Newcomb. While there, I began working as a reporter at the *Times-Picayune*.

The house, when I lived there, was the home of Adele Monroe Williams, widow of George E. Williams, who had purchased the building in 1946. She lived there with her daughter Adele, "Sister," while I was in residence. Her son Herbert Williams fondly recalled the time he spent there before he married his wife, Noel. "You know, we never lived more than a few blocks from Commander's Palace," he commented while recounting the various addresses of his relatives. The Monroe clan (and yes, there is a Clan Munro and they, and their Scots connections, are all active in it) of Adele's generation boasted a remarkable set of sisters, all clever and with interesting personalities. "Well, besides Mother, there was Kitty Westfeldt, and Marion Chambers, and Gertrude Logan, and Alice Labouisse—don't forget Aunt Alice, she was a big socialist and had pictures of Norman Thomas on her walls."

Herbert Williams remembered that, when they moved in, there was a family of small children next door, and, of course, the cemetery. "Mother said she never thought she'd be caught between the quick and the dead." Wit must be a family trait: the writing connection in the Monroe family today is great-nephew Michael Lewis. There were many Monroe literary lights, including famed journalist and nephew Bill Monroe, Jr., who was moderator on *Meet the Press* for many years.

My own tenuous literary contribution comes via the cemetery. Unlike today, it was then in such poor condition that urchins would offer to "show you the mummy" for a nickel and point out a mummy-shaped coffin peeking out of a collapsing wall tomb, or oven. Once, a falling piece of a tomb actually killed someone trying a Halloween prank. I managed to get a newspaper assignment to do a feature story on the cemetery, and thus became the resident expert. When a grave was desecrated and a corpse beheaded, the story was mine. The missing head, or skull, never turned up, but for weeks it was talked about in the newsroom.

One other reporter was, I believe, listening. Jim Conaway, then doing police reports, was at work on a mystery novel set here. Sure enough, a missing head appeared in the plot. The book was a good beginning for Conaway—now Washington-based and a much-published author—but it was the title that had staying power. *The Big Easy* was what he named the book—a term I, for one, had never heard applied to New Orleans before, and for which I am happy to give him credit. Columnist Betty Guillaud picked up the phrase, and it spread from there.

I think Fitzgerald would approve.

Deconstructing the Big Easy

SOMETIMES A NICKNAME is so apt, so perfect, that it fits like a glove: the way the "the Big Easy" has become synonymous with New Orleans.

Tracking the term "the Big Easy" provides a happy, if rambling, stroll through New Orleans memory—the way following a walking club on Mardi Gras Day can give you a skewed city tour.

Is it an old term?

"'The Big Easy'? That's a modernism," local historian Sally Reeves says—and certainly she is about as familiar with historic New Orleans as anyone alive is likely to get. The city's founder, Bienville, can be credited with "Crescent City," but he never called it "le Grande Façile."

There is no listing under that name in *New Orleans Jazz: A Family Album* written by Al Rose and Dr. Edmond Souchon in 1967. Neither Bruce Raeburn of the Hogan Archive of New Orleans Jazz at Tulane University nor jazz historian Jack Stewart could immediately recall any early dance hall or club named "the Big Easy." ("But if I do think of something, I'll let you know," Stewart promised.)

Then there was columnist Jill Jackson—a regular contributor to the *Rider's Digest* on the old New Orleans public service streetcars in the 1940s and 1950s. Did she invent the term?

Jill Jackson turned out Hollywood gossip columns until her death in her nineties. Did she coin the phrase "the Big Easy"? Absolutely not, Jackson insisted when I asked her: "That's after my time."

Columnist Betty Guillaud popularized the phrase. "That's all there is about me on Google!" Guillaud said. She wrote for the *States-Item* and later the *Times-Picayune* beginning in the late sixties. When did she begin using the local term? "It was about the same time they started calling New York 'the Big Apple.'"

James Conaway. Photo courtesy of James Conaway.

In fact, there doesn't seem to be any reference to "the Big Easy" prior to 1970.

That's the year author James Conaway published his novel *The Big Easy*. The book follows the adventures of a police reporter (which Conaway had been at the *Times-Picayune*) through the underside of New Orleans, with crime, drugs, and racial disturbances scattered through the pages.

Did the name exist before Conaway's book?

There is an Internet site maintained by word researcher (and Manhattan traffic court judge) Barry Popik (www.barrypopik.com) that carefully records all possibilities of occurrences of "Big Easy" and finds three, all for New Orleans dance halls and none as a nickname for the city.

Was the phrase used elsewhere in connection with the city of New Orleans?

A digital search of the *New York Times* for 156 years finds Conaway's *The Big Easy* mentioned in a review of top crime novels in that paper on December 6, 1970. From 1851 until then, there had been twenty-nine uses of "the big easy," but none connected with the words "New Orleans." From 1971 to 2004 there were five mentions of "the big easy," all with "New Orleans" and all made after the movie with the same name was released.

So where did Jim Conaway get the phrase "the Big Easy"?

Well, like any good reporter, Conaway just made note of something he heard on the street. Conaway, originally from Memphis, had gone to Southwestern University and the University of North Carolina at Chapel Hill and had been a Wallace Stegner Fellow in Creative Writing at Stanford University when he was hired as a reporter for the *Times-Picayune*, arriving in town two days before Hurricane Betsy in September of 1965. "I was an English major—I thought I'd have to teach English or sell insurance. Journalism saved me," he explained. His first day at work began the morning after the hurricane hit.

Conaway soon became a police reporter. "It was a noir experience—real life noir—although I didn't realize it when I was having it," he said. The world of criminal court at Tulane and Broad was fascinating. "Bigger-than-life characters, a lot of corruption but a lot of freedom," he said. "People could do exactly what they wanted."

He often rode the bus and walked from Claiborne Avenue to the courthouse, an adventurous route. "Once [*Picayune* editor] George Healy saw me walking. He screeched to a stop and made me get in the car! He just didn't get it," Conaway noted.

It was while walking that he overheard two black men use the phrase "the big easy," perhaps describing the city as a place where any musician should be able to succeed with ease. "I was really struck by the phrase 'the big easy.' It was one of those things. You hear something sometimes, and then it sort of goes away. It was only later that it came back to me," he said.

In the book, the phrase is used as an explanation for the city's lack of riots in the 1960s. "The Big Easy's just ten years behind the rest of the world, that's all. You might say it's just too goddamn hot to riot," one character says. There is a racial disturbance in the book, not similar to the New Orleans Black Panther incidents, which occurred just after its publication.

Conaway would complete *Judge: The Life and Times of Leander*

Perez in 1973 and a novel, *World's End,* with a local setting—and an explosion at the Boston Club as a plot device—in 1978. Here his New Orleans writing ended.

On one of his last days at the *Times-Picayune,* Conaway recalls that veteran police reporter "Jack Dempsey had a little piece of paper and he put it on my desk. He said 'You might want to look into this.' I opened the piece of paper and it had David Ferry's name written on it." Ferry would be one of the characters in District Attorney Jim Garrison's odyssey into the Kennedy assassination.

By that time Conaway was gone. He and his wife, Penny, left New Orleans after two years, went to Europe, and eventually settled their family in Washington, D.C., where he later served as editor of *Preservation* magazine of the National Trust for Historic Preservation.

In 1987, the film *The Big Easy* appeared, with a completely different story from Conaway's novel. "I talked to my attorney, but he said it's difficult to sue about a title, especially if the plot is different," Conaway said. Ironically, his *World's End* title was also used by others.

Among Conaway's best-known works are *The Texans,* chronicling well-known citizens of that state; *Napa: The Story of an American Eden,* on Californians; *The Smithsonian: 150 Years of Adventure,* a biography of that institution; *The Kingdom in the Country,* an exploration of today's American West; and his own autobiography, *Memphis Afternoons.*

His newest book, *Nose: A Novel,* tracks wine connoisseurs on a quest, but one recent work, *Vanishing America: In Pursuit of Our Elusive Landscapes,* includes magazine pieces and some new writing. In it he has a New Orleans essay, "The Big Uneasy," reflecting on his years in the city and comparing his hurricane experience of forty years ago with the tragedy of Katrina. He writes: "Insight may be the ultimate service provided to us all by a city older, more interesting, and more enduring than most."

Insight, yes. But inspiration, too!

The Basement Book Shop

Just across Broadway from the old Newcomb College campus, at 7221 Zimple Street, there long stood a vacant yellow building. It was only one room wide, maybe three rooms deep, and had a few weatherboards missing. There was little to hint that this was once a major literary mecca of the South.

When the Basement Book Shop and its proprietor, Tess Crager, were in their prime, this was a literary force to be reckoned with. Tantalizing guest lists for autograph parties, memorable anecdotes regarding famous authors, almost as many stories as there were volumes on the shelves—the Basement Book Shop was special, and in its day, just being there was a pleasure.

Tess Crager was born in 1899 and died in 1985. She grew up in Clinton, Louisiana. She remembered that her parents, when shopping in New Orleans, would bring home books for children and also some for themselves, which were "inappropriate for tender eyes." Those were the ones she would read. "I learned a great deal about life from reading those books," Tess later said.

She graduated from Newcomb College (sometimes roller-skating to its pre-1920 Garden District campus), having earned a degree in English, and was elected to Phi Beta Kappa. She studied at Columbia University in New York for a master's degree. According to her daughter, sculptor Gretchen Sharpless, Tess's literary acumen was not accompanied by practicality. "She had to write home from Columbia to ask for a needle and thread—she had no idea how to buy any."

After working in publishing and for a bookstore in New York, Tess returned to New Orleans where she met and married Robert Crager, who was then in the sales department at the *New Orleans Item* newspaper (where Tess also once worked as a reporter). By the 1930s the Cragers were bookshop owners.

According to Betty Wisdom, who worked at the shop in the late 1950s, the Cragers bought the bookstore business from two sisters, who had given the establishment its name (presumably from a prior location). The Cragers were determined to stick to the shop's proven formula. "When she bought that shop she just took up all the systems they had used. I discovered later on they were not very good systems. She said, 'Oh no, that's the way the girls always did it,'" Ms. Wisdom remembered. For a long time it worked very well.

In the front room of the shop was the lending library. As Ms. Sharpless noted, "It was a wonderful thing to have a lending library, especially during the Depression—people could borrow a new book and read it for fifty cents." There was a large table displaying the library books, shelves for fiction and nonfiction, and under the table were the puzzles for rent. "They were wooden jigsaw puzzles, quite expensive," Ms. Sharpless recalled. Grace Morris, a happy former bookstore customer, remembers those puzzles. "They had the most satisfying click when you put a piece in. I remember we used to do them on the back porch." Joe Morris, Grace's brother, remembered renting science fiction books there as a child, and being surprised they were available at such a "genuine literary establishment."

New books were in the back room. Actually, it was difficult to get new books on the shelves as Tess could not bear to let things go, even volumes that went unsold for ages. What she specialized in was finding just the right book for the right person. Tess was never one to hide her opinions on reading matter. Ms. Wisdom recalled, "If someone ask for a book she didn't like, that irritated her." But she was very patient with "the people whom she cared about, especially the ones who had come in as children."

The Basement Book Shop often set up displays for school "book week" celebrations, when children's books could be ordered at a small profit for the school. And, of course, the Basement Book Shop was where students went for their summer reading assignments. Ms. Wisdom remembered that "John Gunther's book about his son, *Death Be Not Proud*, was always the shortest book on the list and hordes of schoolkids came in for it."

Besides selling and renting books, the Basement Book Shop also published books. "It was my father's idea more than my mother's to go

The Basement Book Shop, authors Betty Carter and Hodding Carter with Tess Crager. Photo courtesy of Louisiana Division/City Archives, New Orleans Public Library.

into the publishing business," Ms. Sharpless noted. "The firm began because when Lyle Saxon was dying they promised they would keep his books in print." Their authors included Robert Tallant and John Chase, whose *Frenchmen, Desire, Good Children* was, according to Ms. Sharpless, inspired by her father.

The Basement Book Shop was also known for its parties, usually for an author with a new book out. "Tess was a celebrity chaser," Ms. Sharpless said. And she caught some spectacular ones: Gertrude Stein and Alice B. Toklas came as a couple, Thomas Wolfe and William Shirer were both entertained, Harnett Kane was a regular, Hodding Carter and his wife, Betty, were honored with a signing. In fact, most local writers and many nationally known ones came to Tess's parties. The only exception was William Faulkner: "she could never get him to show up," commented Ms. Sharpless.

No matter who the visiting star was, Tess Crager was the personality most identified with the Basement Book Shop. Tess was not "all sweetness and light," Ms. Wisdom noted. "She was sharp, bright, and funny and told the most wonderful anecdotes about people she had known." Tess was active in the Tulane Lyceum Association, bringing speakers to campus, and she was a popular speaker herself. "The thing that most impressed me was the fact that she could get up and do a book review without even thinking," Ms. Sharpless admiringly recalled.

Feisty and opinionated, Tess Crager also had clout with the New York publishing world, as a literary agent representing local authors. "When we would go to New York we were treated like royalty—Bennett Cerf himself would take us out to fancy lunches," Ms. Sharpless said.

Unfazed by the famous, the Basement Book Shop's mistress set her own course. "Tess never discriminated. It just wasn't in her," Ms. Wisdom said. "She was set in her ways. She never had bags; it was always 'we can wrap it up for you.' She hated paperbacks." And it might be said that Tess was never domesticated: "she never went shopping—all our groceries came from Miss Lucy at Vonderhaar's," Ms. Sharpless remembered. After her husband, Robert, died in 1957, Tess carried on with the shop. Her daughter Deirdre Stanforth would write *The Brennan's Restaurant Cookbook* and this was a success for the publishing company, but it finally closed and its titles went to Pelican Publishing Company, Inc.

Finally, on the last day of 1981, the Basement Book Shop closed. But its legacy continued. As Betty Wisdom noted, "One of the loveliest things about working at the shop was that Tess let you take home and read whatever you liked." The part of her job she liked best? "I unpacked things." And, she added, "I always loved packages, and packages of books are the very best of all."

Panic in the Streets *Remembered*

IN NEW ORLEANS we are getting a little blasé about the movies. Because of some smart tax laws, the state has a big-time film industry. Just last month, I could walk around the corner from my house and see Harrison Ford between takes in a science fiction production.

It may seem odd, but including this movie essay in the literary section makes sense: it won an Academy Award in the Motion Picture Story category in 1951. Moviemaking is a thriving New Orleans industry today, but having a big-time motion picture made on the streets of New Orleans was an event back then. And, when director Elia Kazan was also cofounder of the Actors Studio in New York and a major proponent of "method" acting, and had a cast largely made up of local people—what resulted captures New Orleans as it looked and sounded mid-twentieth century.

Panic in the Streets fits into the film noir category. Photographed in black and white, it tells a dark story. *Panic* was made the year before Kazan's celebrated film of Tennessee Williams's play *A Streetcar Named Desire*. While *Streetcar* was mostly filmed on a Hollywood soundstage and has only a few New Orleans scenes, *Panic* was filmed totally on the streets of the French Quarter and along the riverfront.

Panic's story, credited to Edna and Edward Anhalt, would receive an Oscar at the 1951 Academy Awards. In these days of bioterrorism scares, it sounds remarkably familiar. An illegal immigrant is shot by a local hoodlum (Jack Palance) and dumped in the river by his sidekick (Zero Mostel). When the body is found and autopsied, it is discovered the man had pneumonic plague, and a public health officer (Richard Widmark) is notified. With the help of a police detective (Paul Douglas), Widmark ignores his own wife (Barbara Bel Geddes)

The Washing Well, where scenes were set in *Panic in the Streets*. Photo by Carolyn Kolb.

for the few days it takes to scour the city to track the victim's path and find those he infected, catch the murderer, and stop an epidemic. And, of course, they do.

The real star of this movie is New Orleans and its people. There are the longshoremen on the docks and in warehouses, moving huge stalks of bananas and sacks of coffee on conveyer belts. There are seamen shown at shape-up in a hiring hall as maritime jobs were doled out. There's a multinational freighter crew and a surly towboat operator. Kazan captures them all, and perhaps at the same time he's keeping images in mind that he will later use in *On the Waterfront*.

The French Quarter in 1950 was part seamy nightclub area and part neighborhood. Kazan catches that flavor, too. And he uses local people for a large part of his cast. Some, no doubt, are just shown going about their daily jobs—a number of New Orleans policemen play themselves in this movie. Kazan also used local actors, many from Le Petit Theatre du Vieux Carré.

The late Mildred Fossier, once head of the city's Parks and Parkways Department, and prior to that the Health Department, was a young actress at Le Petit when she was cast in the film. Her big scene was at the coroner's office in the courthouse at Tulane and Board. "I had one line, and I got paid forty dollars. That was good money, then," she remembered. "I was supposed to dress like a floozy, so I got a fur coat, and I was to be escorted to the morgue to identify a body—'Yeah. That's him' was my line." A policeman took her down the hall. "He was the most polished little man I'd ever seen, from his shoes to his hair. And we'd walk down this corridor outside, and then down the hall. And we had to do it over and over." The retakes were caused by inmates at the next-door Orleans Parish Prison. "They would sing with their morning chores—it was beautiful singing. But then they found out about the movie and they all wanted to audition. So Mr. Kazan stood there and let them sing for him."

According to his autobiography, *A Life*, Kazan wanted to shoot on location to convey a sense of openness and place, and he experimented with this technique on *Panic*. He wanted this to be a film "a deaf man could follow," so he let the camera tell the story. At the same time he worked closely with Richard Murphy, the scriptwriter. Murphy would later say that "not a single line of dialogue was left unaltered." Kazan said they "rewrote every scene every day" and the effect was a naturalness of dialogue that gave the movie a documentary feel. Kazan apparently took to the French Quarter atmosphere, calling making this film "a liberation." He even claimed to have "emptied a whorehouse of its girls" for extras in one scene.

Kazan's film crew themselves left a few location memories. The Washing Well Laundryteria on Bourbon Street at Dumaine was used for several scenes in the film and looks much the same today. The movie company paid a hundred dollars for one night of filming, then balked at paying for the second night, but ultimately did. It is well remembered that the crew ate all of the Tom's crackers in the counter jars and didn't pay for them, while the set designer complained about the background clothing changing as people picked up their dry cleaning.

The Hollywood actors are also remembered. Jack Palance's menacing character, Blackie, operated the Washing Well as his day job. Palance, it is said, was a young actor so unsure of himself he would weep with uncertainty between takes. Zero Mostel, cast as a cringing small-time hood, was called on to run down the street for one nighttime scene—the pudgy Mostel had onlookers concerned for his health as he sweated and panted after repeating his run. Mildred Fossier was so taken aback by Richard Widmark ordering her out of a chair so he could put his pants on it, "I never went to see another one of his movies."

Fossier wasn't the only one on the set with "attitude." The late Le Petit photographer Arthur Tong was fond of telling how he was so intent on delivering some unrelated photos to Gallier Hall during filming that he had a confrontation with Kazan—who promptly gave him a thirteen-line role and a screen credit as a "Lascar Boy" in the freighter scene (which Tong nearly steals with his rendition of a request for "shish-ka-bob" by a stowaway.)

Judy LaBorde remembers that her late brother Jerry as a seven-year-old was cast as the boy who first finds the body of the plague victim. "He had to get a Social Security card—that was a big deal at the time," she said. Her father, a carpenter, worked on some of the movie's sets.

LaBorde's memories of the French Quarter make it obvious why Kazan would want to film there. "It was European—it was so relationship based. You had a relationship with the grocer, with the butcher, with your neighbors. The social texture was just so deep."

As Kazan remembered his time filming *Panic in the Streets,* he commented, "There was no tension anywhere . . . mostly because I was so clearly enjoying myself." Kazan would find tension enough in years to come when his testimony naming names to the House Un-American Activities Committee caused many in the film community to shun him. Much later, he would be honored by the Motion Picture Academy, and, tellingly, many in the audience refused to applaud him.

On film however, his offbeat valentine to the city of New Orleans still does him—and us—proud.

The Times-Picayune: *An Elegy*

In late May of 2012, New Orleans was dealt a tremendous blow: the owners of our newspaper suddenly decided that we no longer needed a daily paper and could make do with a three-day-a-week one. The plan was to go into effect later in the year.

As I write this in June of 2012, I cannot remember a day in my life when I did not have the *Times-Picayune* to read.

When I was little, the paperboy left it at the end of the sidewalk—eventually my father had someone build a little wooden box on a post for it, and there it was placed, neatly folded. He would bring it in, and he and my mother would drink their coffee and read it, each with a favorite section.

I followed the comic strips. Dagwood and Blondie, Nancy and Sluggo, Mandrake and Narda—the cartoon couples were always there, and as they lost popularity they were relegated back to the want-ad section, or they lost their big color panels on Sunday. I was a faithful reader wherever they moved.

I have always liked to read the paper on the floor. This method is not usual, I know. If you read this way you may have to shoo off the cat, but you do not have to fold and refold the pages, and you can spread it out to see an entire "double-truck," as it is called, meaning opposing pages spread out.

One of the advantages of this reading method became apparent when our daughter, Pherabe, was little more than a toddler. She and the paper and I were all on the kitchen floor and I was perusing a huge ad for the K&B Drugstore. She crawled on the paper and pointed triumphantly at the logo, announcing, "KAYBEE!" I do not know how children ordinarily catch the knack of reading, but I have watched it happen, courtesy of the *Times-Picayune*.

My husband is the one who clips things. He still collects newspa-

The *Times-Picayune*, now located at 3800 Howard Avenue. Photo by Carolyn Kolb.

per stories and bundles them to send to our children. When they were in high school, he clipped out each mention of their names in the paper, and our son, Kenneth, has a file of all his sports accomplishments, neatly boxed.

We saved the clippings about us—including my engagement photo, from the days where there would be only one used on a day. Occasionally, we would be photographed at parties. A man named Monk Simon, who worked for the D. H. Holmes Department Store, would send you clippings about yourself. And the *Times-Picayune* would sometimes send you an envelope with pictures they had used: the photographs would have white paint on them to make them appear better in print.

I knew very early on that I wanted to be a writer, and I practiced whenever I could. I wrote for the school newspaper in high school, and I even had a job at the *Bogalusa Daily News*, mostly consisting of typing, but I was one of those who worked on collecting and writing biographies of every one of my classmates when we graduated from high school, and this material made it into print.

In college, I majored in English, but I did manage to take one journalism course, at Tulane. (My college was Newcomb, then the women's college of Tulane University, but we could cross-register for courses.) My journalism teacher was George Simmons, who had been a working reporter, I think at the *Christian Science Monitor*. His wife was the book editor of the *Times-Picayune*.

It was a good elemental course: we focused on clear descriptive writing and an orderly presentation of facts. I remember one assignment in which we were given an Associated Press wire-service text of a speech and had to write a news story from it. It was the farewell address of President Eisenhower, a man not given to short sentences, and making a story from that speech was a trying exercise.

My first job after college was with an oil company; then I worked for WDSU-TV in the promotions department, which I thoroughly enjoyed, but since my husband had a similar job at WWL-TV, a competitor, I looked for something else to do. Finally, before I had been out of school two years, I was hired as a city desk reporter at the *Times-Picayune*.

The *Picayune*, in those days, was located on Lafayette Square, and it had been in that vicinity from the early nineteenth century. It was rather old-fashioned, to put it mildly. The press men actually wore caps, like folded boats, made from newsprint so they could keep ink out of their hair. Reporters were paid in cash, in an envelope, every Friday. I was told that it was because reporters always wanted to go out and gamble on payday, a hobby I never acquired.

There was a large newsroom, and on one side was the *Times-Picayune*, and on the other the *States-Item*, the afternoon paper. There were still editions throughout the day: I remember there was the Final, and the Bulldog, and something called the Bullpup. *Picayune* editions ended with the one printed around midnight and delivered early in the morning. *States-Item* editions started around 9 a.m. and ended with one around 4:30 p.m. that people bought on their way home from work.

In the *Picayune* ladies room, there was an older woman in a uniform who was there on duty all day. I was told that she was the last lady-pressman left from the women who had worked during World War II, and this was a job they created for her. There was one reporter, Albert Goldstein, who had been at a defunct paper, the *New Orleans*

Item, and he was the only reporter who had ever belonged to a union. Albert (his name was pronounced al-BAIR, in the French way) had also worked on the *Double Dealer* literary magazine in the 1920s.

The art critic was Alberta "Rusty" Collier. It was said that once she got so mad at an editor she threw her typewriter out the window. The medical affairs reporter was Podine Schoenberger. She was very bright and won a lot of awards, and she wore showy hats.

Charles L. "Pie" Dufour was a columnist, and he was also a local historian. When the book department had its end-of-the-year sale of new books that had not been given to reviewers, he saw me picking up my little stack of books to purchase and immediately took out a ruler and began to hit my hands: he mistakenly thought I was taking HIS books.

The big-time female political reporters were Iris Kelso and Rosemary James. They got the juicy political stories and knew all the politicians. The police reporter was Jack Dempsey, a jovial fellow I got to know better at the Press Club, which my husband and I joined. It had a bar/restaurant clubhouse on Chartres Street. I actually served as secretary of the Press Club, and wrote songs for the annual satirical Gridiron Show. I did decline to be a chorus girl in the show—the main performance requirement being to appear in a black leotard and tights with one of the letters of G-R-I-D-I-R-O-N affixed to one's rear.

One of my stories received an award in the annual Press Club contest: the one on the Krewe of Zulu's Mardi Gras parade. As a city desk reporter, I covered almost anything: luncheon speeches, press conferences, interviews with visiting dignitaries (I interviewed both A. Philip Randolph and Coretta King), movie reviews, fish kills, and everything in between. Reporters always went out with photographers, because they had cars. One of the photographers moonlighted by selling crime photos, and he was always taking detours to crime scenes. You could invent topics for yourself: I did a three-part feature on high school guidance counseling, and one on a decaying cemetery.

I did not really know the upper levels of the hierarchy at the paper. George Healey was the editor, but other than telling me "don't be cute" when he hired me, and refusing to pay me more than fifteen dollars for a magazine feature I thought was worth more, I had little to do with him. Arthur Felt was the managing editor, and his daughter was a friend of mine, but I seldom saw him.

I worked on the city desk, and the city editor was Fritz Harsdorff, a skinny Texan with a nice smile, and his assistant or maybe coeditor was Vince Randazzo, who was from New Orleans, and had a gruff manner but a good sense of humor. Vince worked Saturdays, and so did I, and so did my fellow reporter Don Lee Keith. Don Lee was from Mississippi and was droll and a very good writer. Another Saturday veteran was Jim Conaway, until he became a police reporter. Conaway was writing a novel at the time, and would go on to more books in the future.

Saturdays could be dull, so Vince would give us things to do. Memorize the sixty-four parishes of Louisiana. Learn the names of the New Orleans legislators. Write obituaries. At Christmas, we also had to write stories for the Doll and Toy Fund, about poor little children and their need for toys. We cheerfully made them up.

Every journalist longs for a great story. Mine came in September of 1965 with Hurricane Betsy. We lived uptown in the lower apartment in a duplex. For the night of the hurricane, we had a full house of people for a dinner party. The wind raged, the roof blew off, the rain came in. In the morning, those of us who had to get downtown set out, dodging downed trees. I got to the *Picayune* on time.

The presses had a generator, but the lights were out in the rest of the building. Since we had manual typewriters (and cigarette-strewn floors: smokers never had ashtrays) and we could open the windows, we just set to work. Some telephones worked, others didn't. The Coke machine lost refrigeration and we drank hot Cokes. Don Lee and I eventually walked toward Canal Street for lunch, and Serio's Delicatessen was making free sandwiches since their refrigerators were off. We dodged power lines and broken plate glass.

My first assignment that day was to cover the city hall press conference. I walked there. When I came up the front steps, I was greeted by Sunny Schiro, Mayor Vic Schiro's wife. She was pushing an industrial-sized broom. And she recognized me. "Carolyn, the windows blew out. We have to get this glass out of the way," she said, and pointed me to a broom. We cleaned the floor in time for the conference. The next morning, every reporter who had come in to work had a byline on the front page, so at least people would know we were safe.

In Betsy, the *Times-Picayune* could print and deliver papers. St. Bernard Parish and Gentilly, the Ninth Ward and the Lakefront had flooded. New Orleans is a geographic bowl, and when water comes in, the bowl fills. But in Betsy, the dry part of the city could still function, and we had readers out there who needed their news, even if some of our reporting staff could not get in to work because of flooding. Everyone who could come in, worked. We went six weeks without a day off, and we arrived early and we stayed late.

It was an exhausting time, but it was one of those times when being a reporter really mattered. Power was out, television sets and radios might not work, but we could still put out a newspaper. We filled a basic need, and there is a great pride in doing that.

Years later, *Picayune* reporters managed to get through Katrina. Without a press, in a flood, headquartered in another town, they managed to report to their readers, and they earned a Pulitzer Prize for their coverage.

Cutting the *Times-Picayune* to three days a week is a heartbreaking thing to do to New Orleans. I will never believe that this cruelty was necessary. I regret it immensely.

Literature Bibliography

If you go to Amazon.com and type in "New Orleans" in the book section, you get more than twenty-six thousand hits. Obviously, there are an incredible number of words expended by writers inspired by New Orleans, or influenced by it, or who set their fictional characters here, or who simply live here. This is what you might call a good book town.

These are my recommendations if you are considering starting a New Orleans collection, or if you are in need of inspiration for leisure reading.

Lick your finger and start turning pages.

Nonfiction

One of the best ways to immerse yourself in New Orleans is to browse through Lyle Saxon's WPA Federal Writers' Project guide to the city. Saxon was an unabashed champion of the city, he always urged folks to mask for Mardi Gras, and his newspaper and magazine features, plus his work mentoring other writers (Faulkner included) and his editing and championing the work of those Depression-era writers who worked under him through the WPA, earn him a special place in the pantheon of New Orleans artists. Plus, this book is a fun read.

Works Progress Administration. 1938. *New Orleans City Guide*. New Orleans: Garrett County Press, 2009.

Getting to know the neighborhoods of the city, their past and their present, is another way of orienting yourself. Campanella is a geographer, and he provides a different vantage point for viewing the city as a whole, including charts and maps.

Campanella, Richard. 2006. *Geographies of New Orleans: Urban Fabrics before the Storm*. Lafayette, La.: University of Louisiana at Lafayette Press.

The nineteenth-century buildings of this city (and a very few eighteenth-century ones) are what give New Orleans its personality. Thankfully, the Louisiana State Museum support group, the Friends of the Cabildo, has published a series of well-written and all-encompassing books explaining styles and building types. This series is a labor of love by a number of hard-working researchers and writers.

Friends of the Cabildo. 1971–1997. *New Orleans Architecture, Vols. 1–8.* Gretna, La.: Pelican Publishing Company.

Maybe New Orleans's idea of Progressive Era reform was a little offbeat, but the legalized prostitution district that existed from around 1897 to 1917 is something anyone would want to know more about. And you get to see some of the E. J. Bellocq photographs of the women involved.

Rose, Al. 1978. *Storyville, New Orleans: Being an Authentic, Illustrated Account of the Notorious Red-Light District.* Tuscaloosa, Ala.: University of Alabama Press.

Biographies: Fascinating Females

You think your in-laws are awful? Michaela Almonester Pontalba's father-in-law, right before doing himself in, shot off some of her fingers. Louisiana inheritance law and the French divorce courts in the mid-nineteenth century are both part of this gripping (and academic) saga of the developer of the Pontalba buildings that ornament Jackson Square today.

Vella, Christina. 1997. *Intimate Enemies: The Two Worlds of the Baroness de Pontalba*, Baton Rouge, La.: Louisiana State University Press.

Whether you like her vampires or her witches or her religious writings, Anne Rice, even when a resident of California, cannot be ignored when you discuss New Orleans books. Get to know her better in this well-done biography.

Ramsland, Katherine. 1991. *Prism of the Night: A Biography of Anne Rice.* New York: Dutton.

This is not exactly a tell-all book, but it certainly gives a gracious plenty of information about one of the more notorious figures in New Orleans in the twentieth century: the well-known madam Norma Wallace. And this is a well-written book by a good writer.

Wiltz, Christine. 2000. *The Last Madam: A Life in the New Orleans Underworld*. New York: Faber and Faber.

Fiction: Novels

There is a magical quality to these three New Orleans novels, each following the saga of a troubled young hero/heroine in the city.

No character in literature is quite like Ignatius Reilly, whose romp through New Orleans has provided me (and countless other readers) with years of laughter. This book catches the spirit of the city on each page, and your library should not be without it. It was a Pulitzer Prize winner in 1981.

Toole, John Kennedy. 1980. *A Confederacy of Dunces*. Baton Rouge, La.: Louisiana State University Press.

Walker Percy, Catholic convert and southern gentleman himself, has drawn a portrait of his character Binx Bolling that not only rings true, but will resonate in your memory. It won the National Book Award in 1962.

Percy, Walker. 1961. *The Moviegoer*. New York: Vintage Press.

This depiction of a young woman in mid-twentieth-century New Orleans is lyrical, but at the same time gives a careful glimpse of her milieu and the limits set around her.

Grau, Shirley Ann. 1961. *The House on Coliseum Street*. Baton Rouge, La.: Louisiana State University Press.

Fiction: Guilty Pleasures

This is an old-fashioned page-turning pleasure of a book, chock full of details about the city and the adventures of several generations of one family.

Keyes, Frances Parkinson. 1942. *Crescent Carnival.* New York: Julian Messner, Inc.

You may not be completely on Anne Rice's wavelength, but you have to at least have a nodding (gnawing?) acquaintance with her vampires. This is first in the series, and is partially set in New Orleans.

Rice, Anne. 1976. *Interview with the Vampire.* New York: Alfred Knopf.

What more could you ask? This detective series stars Benjamin Janvier, free man of color, as hero, with bodice-ripping sensuality, plus political correctness—and the series is set in nineteenth-century New Orleans.

Hambly, Barbara. 1997. *Free Man of Color.* New York: Bantam Books. (There are eight books in the series.)

Fiction: Short Stories

Her novel *The Awakening* is justly famous for its frank depiction of an unconventional late nineteenth-century New Orleans woman. But Kate Chopin's short stories, some published in women's magazines, are taut and well written, and are not stylistically dated.

Chopin, Kate. 1895. *Bayou Folk.* Boston, Mass.: Houghton Mifflin.

Vietnamese immigrants are recently arrived in Louisiana, but they found a voice in these exceedingly good short stories, winner of the Pulitzer Prize for fiction in 1993.

Butler, Robert Olen. 1992. *A Good Scent from a Strange Mountain.* New York: Holt and Winston.

John Biguenet teaches writing at Loyola University, and his craftsmanship is evident in this well-done collection. Biguenet also has used his writing to chronicle and reflect on Hurricane Katrina and its effects. His play *Rising Water* spoke to that.

Biguenet, John. 2001. *The Torturer's Apprentice*. New York: Ecco/Harper Collins Press.

Katrina-Related Books

This passionate account of the lives of Louisiana's shrimp fishermen along Bayou Lafourche and how coastal erosion affects them and impacts the state's future has been updated since it first was published. A must-read if you care about the future of Louisiana.

Tidwell, Mike. 2003. *Bayou Farewell: The Rich Life and Tragic Death of Louisiana's Cajun Coast*. New York: Pantheon Books.

This is a straightforward telling of what happened in Hurricane Katrina, and its aftermath, by the one-time city editor of the *Times-Picayune*.

Horne, Jed. 2008. *Breach of Faith: Hurricane Katrina and the Near Death of a Great American City*. New York: Random House.

Baum's book is a chatty, colorful, and yet sobering account of various New Orleanians, their lives between Hurricane Betsy (1965) and Hurricane Katrina (2005) and how Katrina affected them, by a writer for the *New Yorker*. This is now being crafted into a stage musical.

Baum, Dan. *Nine Lives: Death and Life in New Orleans*. New York: Spiegel and Grau.

PART FOUR

Music

If I tried to think of something that was enjoyable, that always brought a smile to my face, and in which I had a continuing interest, there's no doubt in my mind: it would be New Orleans jazz.

Nineteenth-century New Orleans was the place jazz began. Why here? Well, I believe that New Orleans, in that period, was unique in providing just what musicians needed to bring forth that new music.

New Orleans offered freedom for musicians to experiment with different sounds, inspiration directly from African drum rhythms, a music- and dance-loving culture, immediate access through numerous music publishers to American popular music of the day, and the wealth of musicians and music available, from opera to German brass bands and everything in between.

I was born in New Orleans and lived here until I was four with my mother and my grandmother, and, when he came home from the army, my father. Every weekday morning we listened to WWL radio and *Dawnbusters*. This was a variety show with music and skits. One of the skits involved some country French people—we didn't use the word Cajun then—who lived on Bayou PomPom. The mayor's name was Placide Vidac, and he was always getting in trouble. Oh, how I loved Placide. I loved him so much I named my first doll Placide. The man who played Placide was actually clarinetist Pinky Vidacovich, and his jazz group played on the show.

My own first musical performance was of "Bell Bottom Trousers, Coat of Navy Blue." It was a memorable rendition because I decided to sing it while riding with my grandmother on the streetcar. I think we were in the beauty seats (along the sides at the front), and I suppose it was because I saw all those people seated in lines. They looked like an audience. I had on my sailor suit and I thought it was appropriate. My grandmother must have looked the way most people look when attached to an unattractive child. I recall that she said to our neighbors: "Her father is in the army." I must not have known any army songs.

We moved to Bogalusa, where I went all the way through high school, but we didn't stop listening to WWL, and every Saturday morning the Delta Steamship Lines broadcast a musical send-off for their weekly cruise ship. The band was "Tony Almerico direct from the Parisian Room in the New Orleans French Quarter."

There was one actual jazz musician who lived in Bogalusa and whom I met. His name was Snoozer Quinn and he was a guitarist who played with Paul Whiteman briefly, and with many New Orleans groups, but he died young.

I was one of those children who spend their free time taking lessons, all involved with music. I studied piano, I went to dancing school (I was only good at acrobatics, but I liked wearing costumes for the annual review), I took singing lessons, and even bongo drum lessons from my understanding piano teacher. I taught myself to play the ukulele and then the guitar.

I was a fan of Elvis Presley, I loved rhythm and blues, and I was an enthusiastic, if not skilled, dancer. I collected records: one of my favorites was of New Orleans piano bluesman Champion Jack Dupree's "Shim Sham Shimmy." And, of course, all the New Orleans greats: Fats Domino and Dave Bartholomew, Tommy Ridgley (I danced to him a lot at L.S.U. fraternity parties), and, of course, Little Richard, Smiley Lewis, Shirley and Lee, Deacon John (who is still a great performer). It was, and still is, wonderful music.

When I went to Newcomb, then the women's college of Tulane University, it was just at the end of the era of the beatniks. Oh, how I loved to wear black and go to the French Quarter! One of the people I met there was Dick Allen, who became a good friend. Dick was older than my friend Anne Gavin Cruikshanks and me, so we called him our cousin. Cousin Dick was from Georgia and had worked on his master's thesis at Tulane on the oral history of New Orleans jazz. He was an assistant to Bill Russell, who ran the jazz archive at the library. Mr. Russell lived, surrounded by stacks of papers and records, with his canary and his violin in a little apartment on St. Peter Street. He had come to New Orleans in the 1930s as part of a revival of interest in early New Orleans music. Cousin Dick had come in the 1940s. As part of that revival of interest, some record collectors, fans of early New Orleans music, had formed the New Orleans Jazz Club in 1946.

The New Orleans Jazz Club had a weekly radio show, which I was already familiar with because it was heard every Sunday night at ten o'clock on WWL.

It was at Cousin Dick's suggestion that I wrote a show for the Jazz Club radio program. I chose the history of the first jazz record, made by the Original Dixieland Jazz Band, from New Orleans, in 1917. When the band recorded it in New York, some carpenters in the building thought their new music was so funny they began banging their hammers and tools. They had to record a second time.

One of the great joys of New Orleans music is hearing jazz on the streets. Brass bands don't just play for funerals; they show up everywhere they're hired, and I have heard them with pleasure for years. It was in my college years that I learned to love this, and I happily remember walking through the streets following these bands, and once, during Zulu, walking in the middle of the band because the police dogs doing crowd control were biting people.

After I graduated from Newcomb I worked as a reporter at the *Times-Picayune*. One of the stories I did—actually the last interview he gave—was on an old musician, Papa Jack Laine. He was white, and he had been the manager of a number of brass bands in New Orleans around the turn of the century.

I was lured from my career in daily journalism by a chance to be the director of the New Orleans Jazz Museum. The New Orleans Jazz Club ran the museum in a little house on Dumaine Street just off Rampart. Although I will be the first to admit that being the paid staff with a volunteer board of directors is rather like being caught in the intrigues at the Byzantine Court, I survived it for about two years and had an incredible amount of fun.

One of the pleasures was getting to know musicians such as Edmond Souchon. Doctor Souchon gave me a little banjo pin, which I still treasure. We spent a lot of time talking—well, him talking and me listening, and, even if he was cantankerous at times, he truly loved music, and he truly loved Carnival, especially the Rex Organization.

I got to do a lot of interesting things at the Jazz Museum. I helped put together a multimedia show, with a film made inside a parade, for the Smithsonian Institution, was sent to Philadelphia to serve on a bicentennial commission, and even had a debate on television about whether the 1968 jazz festival would be a success. I said yes, and that it was a good idea to include other types of Louisiana folk music.

One other high point of my time at the Jazz Museum was getting to know a nice musician who had been in New York for years but had come back to New Orleans and was our resident music expert. Danny Barker told wonderful stories and was a good string player, and I remember fondly the hours we spent minding the museum. The museum collection is now at the Old Mint location of the Louisiana State Museum. Traditional jazz's New Orleans story cannot be told without mentioning Preservation Hall. The hall grew out of pass-the-hat concerts that Larry Borenstein organized at his art gallery on St. Peter Street and which I well remember attending.

In New Orleans, we are blessed with good music and we certainly have happy memories of good parties. Actually, I think the first real dancing party I ever attended was for the state convention of the Children of the American Revolution; it was held at the St. Charles Hotel, and Papa Celestin was leader of the band.

After I was married, just listening to music was an excuse to go out—and we used to enjoy Armand Hug when he played piano at the Royal Orleans. What a kind person, and what a good pianist—he had a sweet style and really fine technique.

Another great joy was dancing to jazz, at little dance halls. One we used to frequent was Munster's, on the corner of Laurel and Lyons Street.

There is, of course, another kind of music in New Orleans besides jazz and rock and roll: opera and the symphony. My grandmother was an opera fan. Every Saturday she would listen to the Metropolitan Opera broadcast, and sometimes I would be there, probably playing jacks on the floor, but I remember listening—for some reason it was *The Flying Dutchman* I recall best, probably because it was a sad story.

When I was at Newcomb I went to the opera myself, and I think I heard Placido Domingo early in his career (which basically began in New Orleans)—I also heard him at the gala for the opera put on after Hurricane Katrina. I am a Mozart aficionado: luckily New Orleans has put on some stirring *Don Giovanni* productions and one of *The Magic Flute* I particularly prized.

And I was at the concerts for the last season of the Louisiana Philharmonic Orchestra conducted by the late Klauspeter Seibel—he played the last symphony of a composer for each of the programs. (The orchestra is still a marvel under Carlos Miguel Prieto.)

In New Orleans, there is a bit of music in every part of the city. Dance halls, ballet stars, music clubs and music stores, opera singers and tap dancers, jazz musicians, piano bars: we are a fortunate city to have so much music for our pleasure. And what we do not have now, we remember with fondness, and we listen to the recordings with tapping toes and smiles.

Tulane's Jazz Archive

"A lot of times people take the present for granted; they only think the past is important," said Eleanor Ellis. "But Dick Allen knew it wasn't going to go on forever."

In the 1960s, Ellis had recently graduated from Newcomb College when she went to work for Allen at Tulane University's Hogan Jazz Archive at the university's library.

"You were supposed to go out and hear music," remembered Ellis. "That was part of the job description, if there was one.

"How could you ask for anything better?" she added.

In that ideal job, Ellis worked as a research assistant in an innovative program sponsored by the Tulane history department and housed in the school's library. When the William Ransom Hogan Jazz Archive began at Tulane University in 1958, it was a novelty to think that New Orleans music and musicians could be a scholarly topic. The aim was to record the history of this local folk music. Jazz's home was here—but was much of this rich heritage of music being lost?

Housed today in the library's Jones Hall, the archive started when William Ransom Hogan was a professor in Tulane's history department. He was named administrator of a grant from the Ford Foundation setting up the project.

One of the staunchest fighters in the struggle to preserve New Orleans's musical legacy was the late Richard B. Allen, then a history graduate student. Hailing from Milledgeville, Georgia, he had arrived in New Orleans with trombone in hand. Back in Georgia in retirement in 2005, he said, "I never really played, I just took lessons." He listened closely, he began to love the local music, he at one point had a record shop—and then he discovered his true talent. He was a born interviewer. Once in graduate school he hit his stride, and with Dr.

The Hogan Jazz Archive, Howard Tilton Library, Special Collections, Tulane University. Photo by Carolyn Kolb.

Hogan of the history department and eminent jazz researcher Bill Russell, who had moved here from Chicago, Allen started his work and the archive began.

With a soft Georgia accent, impeccable manners, and a wry sense of humor, Dick Allen set out on his quest to interview as many of the early jazz folk as possible, and to record their memories for the future. Those oral histories are the glory of the archive today—and there are more than two thousand reels of tape of those interviews, not only with the musicians, but also with their families and with jazz fans. And there are sound recordings, films, photographs, books, souvenirs, sheet music, band arrangements, records of the musicians' union (American Federation of Musicians Local 174-496), personal papers, and everything else you could imagine related to New Orleans music. One noted user of Jazz Archive material was documentary maker Ken Burns.

When Eleanor Ellis worked there, the facility was housed in the Howard-Tilton Library on Tulane's campus—now Jones Hall, where, after several moves and name changes of the building, the archive is still housed. The premises today are light and airy, with soundproofed listening rooms and audio and video devices for patrons to use. In the beginning, the office was crowded and storage space was at a premium—but there were good things going on, too.

As Ellis could attest, in the 1960s the archive was also taking note of what was happening on the streets and in clubs and dance halls. Part of the work in those early days was transcribing the interviews, keeping notes on the local music scene, and cataloguing the growing collection of recordings and memorabilia. Trombonist Paul Crawford and Betty Rankin, wife of Professor Hugh Rankin, also worked there in those days. But the most fun was outside the library building.

"Dick Allen would send me out. I would go to the funeral, or parade, and I would take notes: the name of the band, the musicians, their instruments, the occasion and what songs and any other things that stood out. That was really a great part of the job!" Ellis remembered.

Ellis, originally from Amite, Louisiana, is herself a working musician, a blues guitarist and singer in the Washington, D.C. area (check her website at eleanorellis.com).

Music was then, and is now, of paramount importance in the archive.

"You never knew what a day would bring," Ellis recalled, "aside from the fact that your job was to listen to music. All those records were right there in the same room. It was wonderful.

"I used to like to listen to a performer named Richard 'Rabbit' Brown, almost pre-blues, singing 'Times Ain't Like They Used to Be.' I remember listening to the 78, no one had reissued it on an LP—that was a wonderful treat," she added. "And I remember listening to Dr. John's [Mac Rebbenack's] first LP."

Then, and now, the musicians themselves mattered most. "Probably the best thing I took away from that job was knowing the musicians," Ellis added. "It was an opportunity to be around real people who played real music."

As Ellis recalls, in the old days at the archive, "people let Dick Allen know when things were happening—the musicians would call and tell him." Jazz funerals were a regular occurrence. "I don't know that we closed down, but I don't ever remember being made to stay in the office during a funeral," she admitted. All those notes on which band played and which musicians were there are part of the archive, too.

While the interviews continued and the staff took notes on current music, the archive welcomed a myriad of donations including sound recordings, many from the collections of Al Rose, Dr. Edmond Souchon, and Roger C. Gulbrandson (today there are more than 35,000 records, 800 tapes, and 130 recorded cylinders on the shelves). A treasure trove of materials came from Dominic LaRocca, the leader of the first band to be recorded—the Original Dixieland Jazz Band. Photographer Ralston Crawford is represented by over six hundred pictures, and there are files of clippings and films and videos on the shelves. Music and print material came from the Rose and Souchon collections, and many donations were made by William Russell. Orchestrations from the 1890-era Robichaux Orchestra were acquired—and soon were being mined for ideas by the young musicians who flocked to the archive to do research.

In 1980, another graduate student arrived at the archive to work. Bruce Raeburn is now curator and an authority on New Orleans music in spite of the fact that he's a New Yorker. ("Sounds like a salsa commercial, doesn't it—he's from New York?" Raeburn quipped.) "My father was a big band leader and my mom was a jazz singer," Raeburn admits: jazz was in his genes. He still plays drums.

Raeburn noted that the work of the archive has changed somewhat since the early years. Although they still welcome donations (including recorded interviews) and keep up with the current music scene, "we split our time between processing materials and assisting the researchers who come to the archive," Raeburn said.

Work includes making the archive's material readily available on the Internet (jazz.tulane.edu). And transcriptions of those interviews are being scanned and digitized, so that scholars will be able to search for terms and topics in the future.

Journalists regularly use the archive. "Bruce Raeburn and his staff were constantly the source of good information," said Lolis Eric Elie, who "wrote a lot about jazz" as a *Times-Picayune* columnist. Nowadays he makes use of the Hogan Jazz Archive in his script writing for the hit television series *Tremé*. "On the show we are dealing with some of the issues of jazz preservation, and we have called them for that. Their oral histories in particular are excellent. There is information you get there not readily available elsewhere," he pointed out.

A recent scholarly work, *Louis Armstrong's New Orleans* by Thomas David Brothers, of Duke University, used extensive material. Students from Tulane and other area universities make use of the archive—and some of them work as interns learning archival methodology. Jazz tourists come from all over the world, and journalists need information. "A big chunk of my day goes to e-mail reference requests," Raeburn admitted.

Felipe Smith, on the Tulane English faculty, also uses the archive for research into New Orleans's African American performance culture. He appreciates listening to the oral histories. "It comes across better than just having information on a page. If you can actually hear the voices, you get the local flavor of the language."

Raeburn noted that musicians are regular archive visitors. "They could be looking for repertoire—a hard-to-find song. We might have the sheet music or a recording." If a nephew takes over his uncle's band, he might want old photographs or arrangements from the past. A Japanese trombone player wanted help interpreting lyrics on a Bunk Johnson recording. "The singer was probably Creole, with French as his first language. We actually made some progress," Raeburn added.

Raeburn, a musician himself, is also a jazz scholar and author of *New Orleans Style and the Writing of American Jazz History*. He described the theme of his book as "how everybody but the New Orleans jazz musicians themselves defined what New Orleans jazz was.

"We have not been particularly effective in branding our music. We can improve, and take control of how people see our culture," he insisted. At the Hogan Jazz Archive, Raeburn and his staff and patrons are taking a big step in the right direction.

New Orleans Dance Halls

NEIGHBORHOOD DANCE HALLS used to dot the city, offering live music, no cover charge, and a nice choice for a night out on a budget. If I had a favorite dance hall, it would have been Munster's—we used to go on Saturday nights, and Tony Fougerat (with his Kings of Poverty band) had a constantly changing program that kept you on your feet. It was a dingy place, truth be told, but what it lacked in décor it made up in attitude. We were not the only New Orleans couple who appreciated what a dance hall could offer.

"At the dance halls you had really great dancers, men who knew how to dance!" Betty Rousse Glowacki was born in New Orleans in the 1920s and she has loved to dance nearly all the years since, she told me during an interview in 2011. Her husband, Frank, could polka (and had relatives in his home state of Ohio who played in Slovenian polka bands), but Betty Glowacki had different tastes.

"I always loved to dance. I learned to dance real ballroom dancing, and I didn't take lessons," she proudly asserted. A native Orleanian, she was born "at the French Hospital on Orleans Street—it was right where St. Peter Claver is, by the down ramp of the expressway." Her father had died when she was very young, and the man who became her stepfather used "to have me stand on his feet to learn to dance, and my godfather was an excellent dancer, too. I just learned from the family."

"The story of music in New Orleans must begin with dancing," author Henry A. Kmen noted in his *Music in New Orleans: The Formative Years 1791–1841*. By 1805, the town held fifteen public ballrooms, and there were more than eighty by 1841. In the early city, lack of a common language was never a problem when the band struck up a tune.

The American vs. Creole rivalry sometimes meant that a dance

Munster's Dance Hall, at the corner of Laurel and Lyons streets, was located in the rear portion of this building. Photo by Carolyn Kolb.

program included formal French dances as well as American country dancing. General Andrew Jackson and his wife, Rachel, celebrated his victory at the Battle of New Orleans on the dance floor, to the strains of "Possum Up a Gum Tree." During the Civil War, Nathaniel P. Banks, the Union general who took over New Orleans from the controversial Benjamin Butler, tried to soothe the local population and decrease Confederate support by hosting numerous balls and entertainments. Banks was accused by a fellow Union officer of attempting to "dance the fair creoles to loyalty," according to Stephen A. Dupree in his *Planting the Union Flag in Texas: The Campaigns of General Nathaniel P. Banks.*

The spontaneous musical invention that would become jazz provided the rhythms for those dancing Orleanians beginning late in the 1800s. The city's early fondness for public ballrooms translated into a proliferation of dance halls: public places that offered a dance floor and room for musicians. The halls might belong to a fraternal organization, they might be part of a liquor establishment, they might host any number of other public events, but the function of New Orleans dance halls was mainly to provide a stage on which the local populace could perform and enjoy their own company.

Dance halls provided an escape and an inexpensive amusement. As Mrs. Glowacki recalled, "It was the Depression. We lived in one house, all different generations. My divorced aunt, the big thing she did was on Saturday night she would go dancing in this club on St. Claude Avenue, and she would bring me. You just went in, you didn't have to have an escort, and there were always gentlemen who would ask you to dance. It was a lot of fun, always good music, local bands played."

Dance halls might be very spare in their decoration. Describing Luthjens (the first of that name was in the 1200 block of Franklin Avenue, before it burned in 1960), Mrs. Glowacki said, "It was a regular dance hall. You came in, there were tables and chairs, nothing fancy. Just raw wooden tables, maybe even just fold-up chairs. It was a fun place to go on a Saturday night out. You could nurse a beer." Luthjens catered to an older clientele. "The nickname was 'the old folks home,'" she explained.

In its later incarnation at the corner of Marigny and Chartres streets, Luthjens kept up its adult atmosphere. "There was a sign that said, 'No Jitterbugging'—the sign is still across the street at the Friendly Bar,'" music historian Dr. Jack Stewart explained. Were they serious about that rule? "Well, I once jitterbugged in there and they kicked us off the dance floor," Stewart related.

Luthjens in its heyday provided work for a changing number of musicians. Lars Edegran, a Swedish jazz enthusiast (proficient on piano, clarinet, and guitar) and longtime New Orleans resident, led the Luthjens house band in the late 1960s.

Trumpeter Clive Wilson, who arrived in New Orleans in the 1960s from England, has made his living here in music, and has done his share of dance hall stints. "Back in the early 1960s I sat in with the band at Luthjens. I also used to sit in with Kid Thomas Valentine at the Firemen's Hall in Westwego. And I used to sit in with Tony Fougerat at Munster's." Munster's, on Laurel at Lyons Street, had a regular clientele of dancers, and it also functioned as the home base of the Lyons Carnival Club, a walking club.

Musicians find benefits to playing for dancing, Wilson, himself a dancer, admitted. "Regular dance hall dancing is just kind of relaxing" for the musicians. "The music seems to flow, I think you feel better when people are dancing: it feels like your music has some extra purpose." Wilson, who leads the New Orleans Serenaders, also plays with Tommy Sancton at Preservation Hall and at the Palm Court.

Dance halls can be problematic for musicians. With all those dancers in close proximity, accidents can happen, according to Stewart, a regular member of the New Leviathan Oriental Foxtrot Orchestra. "At the Columns Hotel once, a couple fell into the band and onto a music stand and knocked it over," he recalled.

Various solutions to protect the band evolved over the years—rarely, the band ending up playing behind chicken wire in overly rowdy establishments. "The idea is separating the musicians from the dancers," Stewart noted, and he cited the elevated bandstand as the best solution. The Jefferson City Buzzards Hall on Annunciation Street has an elevated bandstand, as one example.

Dance halls still exist in the city, and Luthjens may be in for a rebirth. Marigny resident Julian Mutter actually tried to buy the hall some years ago, after it had gone through a punk rock phase and a quasi-religious phase, but he only acquired it some years later. "It went back on the market and I bought it within twenty-four hours.

"I'd love to bring it back as a music venue for traditional jazz, and private parties. I'm in an awkward position; it lost its nonconforming use status, so it's actually zoned residential. I am going to try and get it put back" into the right zoning classification for live music, Mutter said.

New Orleanians can still find a hall where they can dance away their Saturday night. Rock 'n' Bowl on S. Carrollton Avenue and Southport on Monticello Avenue just over the Jefferson Parish line are dependable dance choices. That classic dance hall, the Old Firemen's Hall at 320 Fourth Street in Westwego, even has its own website, oldfiremenshall.com. And just wait till you have a chance to try out some steps on that springy, wooden dance floor: whatever the music, you can bet that "Jitterbugging Is Allowed!"

Feet First: Male Dancers

FEW OTHER CITIES prize the ability to dance as much as New Orleans does—everyone, male or female, is expected to be able to take to the dance floor at the slightest provocation. It isn't surprising that a number of Orleanians are good enough for the big leagues, that is, skilled enough to be professionals. Those dance pros include a number of New Orleans men.

"Any boy we had in the department who finished the course of study became a professional," Denise Oustalet remembered. From 1976 to 2000 she guided dance students through the New Orleans Center for Creative Arts public high school program, teaching ballet as part of dance studies that included jazz, tap, character, and modern dance. Today, besides NOCCA's dance department, New Orleans can boast numerous other dance education opportunities—but whatever might have been available in the past, New Orleanian males who wanted to dance always found a way.

Joseph Giacobbe, of Giacobbe Academy of Dance and Delta Festival Ballet, said his sisters, Maria and Georgie, had started a dance school, and at six he became a pupil. "By the time I was a teenager, I really knew I was serious." Joseph and his wife, Gwen Delle, met through dancing and have remained partners, both on stage and with the dance academy. Growing up in Metairie, Joseph Giacobbe already had a connection to the late Peter Gennaro, a national dance icon.

"My family knew the Gennaros well. They had the restaurant and bar, close to the end of Metairie Road where it meets Airline Highway, and my father had a grocery store about two blocks away. Metairie was like a little village then," Giacobbe noted.

The elder Gennaro opened his bar and restaurant "the day after Prohibition ended" in 1928, Peter's nephew Jimmy Gennaro said. "They expanded the restaurant for Peter, built a big room for him to

Royes Fernandez in *Don Quixote*. Photo by Jack Mitchell, New York City, courtesy of Jeanne Bruno.

dance—it's still there in the back. But that wasn't enough for him, he had bigger ideas."

Peter Gennaro enlisted in the army in World War II, joined an entertainment troupe in India, and used his G.I. Bill education funds for dance training. He met his wife, Jean Kinsella, when they were dancing for the same company—she and their son and daughter live in New York.

As a performer, Peter Gennaro appeared in numerous Broadway shows including *The Pajama Game* in 1954 and *Bells Are Ringing* in 1956. He was co-choreographer of *West Side Story* in 1957 and won a Tony award for choreography of *Annie* in 1977. His Peter Gennaro Dancers were a television staple of the 1950s and 1960s, appearing on *The Perry Como Show, Your Hit Parade*, and *The Ed Sullivan Show*.

According to his nephew Jimmy, Peter Gennaro had a special difficulty: "He was deaf. He had a hearing aid in one ear, and the other ear was completely deaf.

"I remember we were watching him on *Ed Sullivan* one night and his hearing aid fell out and slid across the floor. But he just kept going.

"He had the rhythm in his blood—that New Orleans thing," Jimmy Gennaro added.

Another Orleanian with fascinating rhythm was classical ballet dancer Royes Fernandez, who died in 1980. His sister Jeanne Bruno noted that "he is the only American 'Danseur Noble'" (an accolade for a male dancer partnering a ballerina, "it's just qualities beyond technique," she explained).

Fernandez and his sister both studied under renowned New Orleans ballet teacher Lelia Haller, who had trained in Paris. Her mother enrolled Jeanne for class, and eight-year-old Royes came along. "He was just very rare, a very rare talent," his sister said.

Fernandez quit dancing as a teenager at Fortier High School. Then, Lelia Haller began doing choreography for opera and asked him to return to the stage. An invitation to summer ballet classes in New York followed, but Fernandez's parents declined to send him there full time. During his senior year, Haller got him an audition with visiting ballerina Alicia Markova. "I went down with him on the streetcar, he did some barre work and at the end of the audition he was invited to join the company," Jeanne Bruno proudly recalled. "He never came back."

Fernandez's primary affiliation from 1950 to 1973 was with the American Ballet Theatre, first as a soloist and then as a principal dancer after 1957. He partnered the best-known ballerinas of his time: Margot Fonteyn, Lupe Serrano, Maria Tallchief, Alicia Alonso. Fernandez was always attentive to his partners: "Whenever he did performing, he and that ballerina would be together the entire day," Jeanne Bruno said. "Yes, he was very handsome, but he was a very modest person, he was an artist. That was his whole life, was dance."

When Fernandez left active performing he taught, and from 1974 until his death was on the faculty of the State University of New York at Purchase.

Fernandez's first stage in New Orleans would have been Dixon Hall on the Newcomb College campus, where Lelia Haller staged recitals. Jeanne Bruno was able to tell that to the dancers when the American Ballet Theatre's Studio Company performed there under direction of another local dancer, Kirk Peterson.

Peterson, whose mother and aunt had danced on stage, also trained with Lelia Haller, and was a principal dancer with the American Ballet Theatre and the San Francisco Ballet. He has choreographed over fifty ballets and also served as ballet master of the American Ballet Theatre.

"On my fourth birthday I announced I was ready for dance class," said George Smallwood. "I was kind of a ham." Smallwood was a senior at NOCCA when the foundation was dug for the school's new riverfront facility, and he later brought Theater Battleworks, a dance company he cofounded, to NOCCA on tour. Smallwood also danced with the Martha Graham Dance Company and joined the Paul Taylor Dance Company in 2011. With his double major in dance and business from Southern Methodist University, Smallwood often manages a New York shop when he is not on stage.

Jason Lacayo also went to S.M.U. for dance and marketing, and was in the companies of both the Los Angeles Opera and Santa Fe Opera and on Broadway in a revival of *Fiddler on the Roof*. He had an on-screen role in *The Producers* in 2005 and danced in the film *Across the Universe* in 2007.

Two African American dancers from New Orleans, Stephen White and Robert McCaskill, were NOCCA dance students and were both semifinalists in the National Arts Recognition and Talent Search, "the Presidential Scholars of the arts," according to Denise Oustalet. White later danced with the Dutch National Ballet. Two other African Americans, Kevin Gaudin and Cornelius Washington, also danced professionally. Gaudin is currently with the Rod Rodgers Dance Company in New York.

Gilbert Rome began dancing at Gayle Parmalee's school here, danced with the National Ballet of Canada and the Houston Ballet, served as choreographer of the City Ballet of Houston, and currently teaches in the Loyola preparatory ballet program here.

As Joseph Giacobbe recalled, "Jerel Hilding had talent, was a musician and a varsity athlete, and he loved to perform." Hilding, a graduate of the University of New Orleans, was a principal dancer with the Robert Joffrey Ballet for fifteen years, and is now associate professor of the University of Kansas dance department.

Patrick Howell is with the Milwaukee Ballet. Tobin Eason is with the main company of the American Ballet Theatre. Richard Rholdon studied at the American Ballet Theatre School and is now ballet master for Delta Festival Ballet.

Harvey Hysell, who had his own school and ballet company here, trained local dancer Ian Carney. Carney, now a partner in Cordian Visual Arts and Dance and Lightwire Theatre, and his wife, Eleanor, were with the Montgomery Ballet in Alabama and now are on the Tulane University ballet faculty.

Maybe it's the music in the air, but when New Orleanians hear that beat, some of them never stop dancing!

The B Sharp Music Club

ONE OF THE TRAGEDIES of Hurricane Katrina in 2005 was the destruction of Pontchartrain Park, a 1950s-era subdivision built near Lake Pontchartrain for New Orleans's African American middle-class families. In 2003, I had met one of the residents, Elise Dunn Cain, when I was researching the B Sharp Music Club. She was a charming woman, proud of her family, and a true music lover. I was horrified when I realized the storm had destroyed her home and her neighborhood. And I wondered what had happened to the club.

Fortunately, Ms. Cain herself is safe, and had moved to Maryland, near her children. And, as I found out from her nephew Dr. Robert N. Perry III, there is still a B Sharp Music Club. "Our membership is small, but we still are active," he explained. He still plays piano and sings in a choir, and is on the faculty of Nunez Community College.

Dr. Perry mentioned that one of the Katrina casualties was his piano, which had been his mother's. "Duke Ellington played that piano; he came to my mother's house when he was in town—and he had some gumbo, too," he recalled.

Perry's mother was one of the Dunn sisters, women destined to have music in their lives. "Well, we were five girls—and we all had to learn to play the piano," Elise Dunn Cain reminisced about growing up in New Orleans as one of the daughters of a Congregational minister. "And there was no question about ARE you going to college, it was just WHEN you go to college," she said firmly. The Dunn girls shared high aspirations (all did become college graduates) and a good, basic musical knowledge. And they also shared membership, with their mother, in a unique musical organization, the B Sharp Music Club, which has been a pride of the New Orleans African American community since its founding in 1917.

The B Sharp Music Club: (from left) Dr. Robert N. Perry III, Beatrice Perry Soublet, Lillian Dunn Perry, (front) Dr. Robert N. Perry, Jr. Photo courtesy of Dr. Robert N. Perry, Jr.

The club was created by a remarkable woman, Camille Lucie Nickerson, who had a music school. Ms. Nickerson, a native Orleanian, was an accomplished pianist and organist, and later would serve as director of the children's department of the School of Music at Howard University, Washington, D.C. She had bachelor's and master's degrees in music from Oberlin Conservatory and was the recipient of a Rosenwald fellowship for advanced study at Julliard in New York. She was perhaps best known as an arranger and interpreter of Creole folk music and appeared in lecture-recitals throughout the country.

The late Lucille Levy Hutton, a charter member of the B Sharp, in a memoir written some years ago, remembered fondly: "One day in February 1917, about twelve of us, advanced pupils of the Nickerson School of Music, met in Miss Nickerson's studio and organized the B Sharp Music Club. Miss Nickerson's purpose in forming the club was to lead her pupils into the wider field of present-day musical thought and to cultivate a finer musical taste," according to Ms. Hutton.

"For two years the club went along very contentedly, meeting twice a month at the Nickerson School of Music. Some of us even yet like to remember those times—a happy combination of study and play."

However, World War I intervened. The girls in the music club noticed they were bringing along their Red Cross knitting projects to the club meetings—could the B Sharp Music Club do something for the war effort? It was decided that a benefit concert could raise funds for a phonograph for the Rest Room, a Red Cross–sponsored gathering place for traveling African American soldiers. Before all the money was raised, an armistice was declared. But the club decided to keep the money and put it to charitable use as needed. Later, funds would go toward music scholarships. And the program of sponsoring concerts continued.

By 1921 the club was growing and Camille Nickerson made a summer trip to a meeting of the National Association of Negro Musicians (which she would later serve as president). She was so impressed with the organization that she suggested that the B Sharp Music Club affiliate. This was done, and the first male members were welcomed—including Charles B. Rousseve (who will be remembered for his book *The Negro in Louisiana*, published in 1937 by Xavier University Press).

The far-reaching aims of the B Sharp Music Club, according to an early constitution found in their archives at the Amistad Center at Tulane University, were:

1. To assist in maintaining a community where all people may live in peace and harmony
2. To spread abroad the love and appreciation of traditional and original Negro music
3. To foster a larger public appreciation for an education in good music as preparation of the advent of real Negro genius
4. To encourage the use of Negro Folk themes as a basis for compositions by Negro composers
5. To resist desecration of Negro spirituals
6. To develop higher professional standards through lectures, conferences, and study meetings
7. To promote the exchange of ideas and the spirit of fellowship among musicians
8. To create wider opportunities for Artists and Musicians

9. To discover, encourage and assist the cultivation of musical gifts among talented, deserving Negro youth and to sponsor such activities as will extend the influence of music as a necessary and inspiring element in the life of the people
10. To establish and maintain a fund for scholarships
11. To assist the National Association of Negro Musicians, Inc., in its scholarship program, its conferences and other activities sponsored by it.

In 1922 the B Sharp held the first monthly "Pleasant Hour," described as a program of "musical numbers, community singing, readings and short talks, presented to the community entirely free." Of the early Pleasant Hours, Ms. Hutton's memoir related that "we have been particularly fortunate in securing local and visiting artists and speakers of both races." In fact, in 1925 two programs featured Helen Pitkin Schertz, a white Orleanian who played the harp (in a duet with Camille Nickerson on organ). Schertz, a writer of New Orleans–based books, was more widely known as one of the founders of the Spring Fiesta Association and of the group that became Le Petit Theatre du Vieux Carré.

Also listed on one of the early programs in a men's quintet was Dr. Andrew Young, father of the former mayor of Atlanta (and "a fine tenor" according to Elise Dunn Cain).

Through the years the B Sharp Music Club sponsored Christmas programs, Mother's Day programs, and Carnival programs, and welcomed performers, both national (such as concert pianist Leon Bates, who is also Elise Cain's son-in-law) and local (including Moses Hogan, Debria Brown, Shirley Verrett, and Irving Mayfield among many others).

There were three types of members in the B Sharp: professional musicians (including music teachers), amateur musicians, and patrons of the arts. Members could be active (and live in town) or associate (and live elsewhere). There were also several types of meetings: regular meetings, business meetings, study meetings, and social meetings. For many years there was a B Sharp Junior Music Club, whose members became B Sharp members upon graduation from college (all the Dunn sisters began as junior members).

There have been very few presidents of the B Sharp Music Club since its 1917 birth: one was Lillian B. Dunn, and one was her daughter, the late Lillian Dunn Perry. Elise Cain remembered her sister fondly, and Lillian Dunn Perry is familiar to many Orleanians as the pianist at New Orleans City Council meetings for many years. The Robert Perry Singers were named in honor of her husband, Robert N. Perry, Jr., who also served as a B Sharp president.

Today the B Sharp Music Club is not as active as it once was, but Dr. Perry pointed out, "We have a lot of performers who are former B Sharp scholarship winners, and they are active musicians." He said the club is planning a membership drive. One hopes that this congenial variation on a musical theme will continue. In the key of B sharp, of course.

Werlein's For Music

I WAS AN OCCASIONAL Werlein's customer. You could always find guitar strings, sheet music, and concert tickets. If you are going to have a musical city, you have to have supplies for the musicians. And having a one-stop shop for instruments, repairs, and even lessons was certainly important to New Orleans's musical heritage. Werlein's served a purpose, and, in many ways, the music store permeated all of our lives.

The deep male voice over the phone intoned the familiar phrase: "Guitars, drums, organs, pianos—everything musical at Werlein's." Then, the caller would hear the time and the temperature.

The voice was the late Philip Werlein's. The phone service was the once-popular "Time and Temperature" number that everyone in New Orleans dialed regularly.

According to his daughter, Bitsie Werlein Mouton (Mrs. Grover Mouton), "It was an advertising medium that reached across all age groups. It would just stop you in your tracks. It was very somber. He had a very deep voice. People to this day talk about it."

Werlein's For Music was a fixture at 605 Canal Street for the better part of a century. Today, the Palace Café restaurant occupies their building (which is still owned by the Werlein corporation). While it had other New Orleans locations before Canal Street, the firm's first home was in Vicksburg, Mississippi.

According to Bitsie Mouton, the founder of the family firm was Philip Werlein "the first," who came over from Germany in the 1840s as a music educator. He was able to ship instruments up the Mississippi River, taught music in Mississippi, started a music publishing business in Vicksburg, then relocated to New Orleans in the 1850s. The firm's scrapbooks and documents are now housed at the Historic New Orleans Collection.

Werlein's For Music's building is now the Palace Café, 605 Canal Street. Photo by Carolyn Kolb.

Werlein's music publishing business continued after the Civil War (the firm had been a publisher of "Dixie"), but it became best known as a source for instruments and music supplies. According to Parham Werlein (Bitsie Mouton's uncle and another long-time member of the firm) in an interview in 2010, the Union Army's occupation of New Orleans resulted in Werlein's store being closed and its stock disbursed. Employees had hidden some of the pianos in a barn, and after hostilities had ceased, that stock provided the start of the reopened business.

Pianos were Bitsie Mouton's specialty at Werlein's. "I play, but I'm not a great pianist," she admitted. Her mother, Anastasia Schlueter Werlein, was a concert pianist—her parents met when her mother, then a college student, played a concert in Shreveport where the young Philip Werlein was working at Werlein's Shreveport location. "She was surrounded by nuns from the college—it was difficult to court her." A long and happy marriage resulted, and on moving back

Werlein's advertisement. Courtesy of Tulane University Louisiana Research Collection.

to New Orleans, Anastasia became the pianist for the local symphony while her husband rose through the ranks at the family company.

Ms. Mouton had worked there during summers in school, but when she was in her thirties, she and her husband, Grover, an architect, came back to New Orleans after years of living in New York and Europe, and she began working full-time at the music store, with a special interest in selling pianos. Werlein's had stocked, among other brands, Mason and Hamlin pianos and then added Steinway pianos to the inventory. The Texas pianist Van Cliburn's parents bought his first Steinway at the Werlein's in Shreveport.

Werlein's customers were loyal—not only to the store, but to their favorite piano. Keith Dockery Derbes (Mrs. Stephen Derbes) said that her mother, the late Keith Somerville Dockery (Mrs. Joe Rice

Dockery) of Dockery Farms, outside Cleveland, Mississippi, had been given a Mason and Hamlin piano from Werlein's by her parents. After her marriage, her husband offered her a Werlein's Steinway, and she suggested they trade in her old piano. Immediately, she regretted her decision, but things were quickly resolved. "For all my childhood, we had two grand pianos in the living room," Ms. Derbes remembered.

Certain occupations also gravitate to the piano. "Great surgeons make great pianists," said Ms. Mouton. "I can't tell you the number of great concert grands I sold to surgeons. Surgeons have some sort of affinity to piano excellence."

Parham Werlein, with fifty-five years at the company working at every level, was knowledgeable about band instruments. A saxophonist himself, he often accompanied bandleader René Louapre, director of instrumental music for Orleans Parish Public Schools, on trips to local schools to demonstrate instruments and encourage youngsters to join the band.

Besides selling instruments, Werlein's also offered music instruction and instrument repair. In the oral histories collected at the William Ransom Hogan Jazz Archive at Tulane University, Werlein's figures in many anecdotes of the early years of the music. The legendary Kid Ory, who grew up in Algiers, was playing in bands at fourteen, when he crossed the river one day in 1900 to visit his sister and go to Werlein's to purchase his first trombone.

As Ory told the story in 1957, he played the instrument at the store, returned to his sister's home on Jackson Avenue at S. Robertson Street, and began to play again. Soon there was a knock on the door. The legendary Buddy Bolden was outside, wanting to give Ory a job. It was not to be: his sister told Bolden her little brother had to stay home until he was twenty-one.

Trumpeter Peter Bocage related that he went to New York around 1920 with Armand J. Piron's band to play recording dates that had been arranged for them by Werlein's. Bocage said they were the first African American band to record for Victor records. An audition for a Broadway hit show, *George White's Scandals*, was purposefully sabotaged by the homesick New Orleans band members, much to Piron's dismay.

The firm was concerned with everything musical. Werlein's at one time in the 1800s had a concert hall, and Werlein's had sponsored the local appearance of Enrico Caruso and later of Paul Whiteman's Orchestra. Parham Werlein pointed out that Werlein's had a large ticket business, with sales for all local musical events. The symphony had its offices on the third floor. Piano recitals were regularly scheduled in the upstairs auditorium, where Les Paul and Mary Ford also once performed. Werlein's stocked sheet music and band arrangements. If you had business with music in New Orleans, you went to Werlein's.

Fats Domino's two Steinways came from Werlein's—and the one damaged in Katrina is now on exhibit at the Louisiana State Museum. Pete Fountain had his clarinets repaired there—and the Assunto brothers (Frank and Freddie) of the Dukes of Dixieland might have done the repair work.

Parham Werlein sold a phonograph and some records to Tennessee Williams—"he said he liked to write with the records on." The Rolling Stones stopped in while in town. Little Harry Connick, Jr., used to come in and play the grand pianos to everyone's amazement. Werlein's was definitely in tune with music in the city.

While the firm once had clients and outlets throughout the region, the nature of the music business was changing, and the last store in Metairie finally closed.

Bitsie Mouton noted that "we brought our company to the proper closing, and the family is happy with what we hope we have contributed. It was special, because New Orleans is so deeply involved with music."

A legacy in which she takes special pride is Werlein's contribution to fostering music for young people. "The very beginning of music is music in our schools, that's where it all begins, and we contributed there.

"Our stores were always filled with kids, with big dreams, and we feel that's an important legacy that we leave, that we helped children all along their way."

New Orleans Opera Stars

New Orleans has been home to an amazing number of talented singers gracing opera stages around the world.

Barbara Faulkner Bernard (1958), Lavergne Monette (1960), Shirley Verrett (1961), Natalia Rom (1979), Jeanne-Michelle Charbonnet (1990), and Elizabeth Futral (1991)—all of these opera singers have New Orleans ties, and all of them enhanced their singing careers through the Metropolitan Opera National Council Auditions, a program dating from 1954.

However, back in 1952, a New Orleans tenor named Caruso tied for first place in what was then called the Metropolitan Opera Auditions of the Air, which began in 1935.

The winning Loyola graduate Charles Anthony Caruso took some advice from the Met's general manager Rudolf Bing, and changed his name to Charles Anthony. In his fifty-seven-year-long career at the Met, Charles Anthony would sing 111 roles in 69 operas. He died in February 2012, as the Met singer with the longest career on stage.

Why does New Orleans produce so many opera singers?

"We have a two-hundred-year tradition of opera in New Orleans, and we have a tradition of great teachers," suggested John Baron, music professor at Tulane. The first opera known to be performed here was André Ernest Grétry's *Sylvain,* in 1796. Gregorio Curto and Julia Calvé Boudousquie, both early singers at the French Opera, became music teachers, beginning a tradition of serious vocal instructors, Baron said.

"New Orleans has always been a city where vocal music was perhaps more important than instrumental music," according to opera aficionado Jack Belsom. And, beginning in the 1930s, Loyola had begun to emphasize voice in their music department, Belsom pointed out, while Xavier University had an important opera workshop into

Norman Treigle as Escamillo in *Carmen*. Special Collections & Archives, Monroe Library, Loyola University. Used with permission of the New York City Opera.

the 1960s. Opera fan Keith Derbes added that Tulane University also has training for singers, and L.S.U. and U.N.O. have music departments, too.

Phillip Frohnmayer, Mary Freeman Wisdom Distinguished Professor of Music and Coordinator of Vocal Performance at Loyola, credits the lifestyle of Orleanians with the production of opera singers. "New Orleans is an opera town. It's not an odd thing to be an opera singer here.

"It has a little to do with dressing up and Carnival, and masks, and it's a little bit more laid-back way of life. It allows singers to give their bodies the kind of relaxation that good singing requires," Frohnmayer added.

"This is a city of performers," Belsom explained.

Frohnmayer noted that "there is a tradition of people who have done it: so a generation can look back at the ones who came before."

Loyola has regularly staged student opera productions since the 1980s. Even the New Orleans Recreation Department used to put on operas: future opera singer Jo Ann Yockey sang the title role in *Madame Butterfly* in 1967. Isidore Newman School had an annual Gilbert and Sullivan performance: the cast of *Patience* in 1960 included future opera singers Michael Devlin and Ruth Falcon. And the New Orleans Opera Association has an annual season of performances.

Opera fans like Keith Derbes enjoy watching young singers as well as polished performances. While she once chaired the regional auditions (including the one won by recent immigrant Natalia Rom, who arrived here from Russia with her extended family), Derbes admits that the performance of the singers on stage is only a part of the spectacle. "The judges come from music schools and opera companies across the country. Someone always gives a master class—singers have one-on-one exposure to a judge, for a little coaching and a little individual attention," she said. And, she admitted, even the local volunteers get involved. "We always enjoyed being able to help the singers go on to New York, if they needed clothes, or anything."

Every January, Loyola University hosts one of fourteen regional finals, this for the Gulf Coast Region, in the Metropolitan Opera National Council Auditions. Young opera singers perform in Roussel Hall, representing their home district: New Orleans, Shreveport, or Mobile, Alabama, or Puerto Rico. Winners in the regionals here will go on to the national semifinals on the stage of the Metropolitan Opera in New York. Ten semifinalists will compete as finalists in the Grand Finals Concert, accompanied by the Metropolitan Opera Orchestra. Five Grand Winners each receive fifteen thousand dollars, other finalists get five thousand dollars, and other semifinalists each receive fifteen hundred dollars to further their studies.

As for the singers New Orleans can claim: everyone has a favorite. According to Jack Belsom, "If I had to choose the two most important ones, I would say Norman Treigle and Shirley Verrett—although she grew up on the West Coast."

Shirley Verrett was a mezzo-soprano who sang at the New York City Opera and also the Metropolitan Opera, and who had close family in New Orleans.

Treigle was a bass-baritone who sang with the New York City Opera. A New Orleans native, he was trained at Loyola and, even during his active career, spent much time in New Orleans, where he was often seen at the fairgrounds. His daughter Phyllis Treigle was also an opera singer.

Treigle, to the regret of some of his fans, never sang at the Metropolitan Opera. It was by choice. As quoted by the *New York Times* in his obituary, Treigle admitted that "the Met was my dream as a kid, but I gradually got it out of my system." As he explained, "When you have a company based on the star system, it's impossible to build the kind of rapport that you need for opera as I conceive it."

Ironically, the Metropolitan Opera must think well of Norman Treigle these days: their online record shop stocks his recording of *The Tales of Hoffman* with New Yorker Beverly Sills (his fellow New York City Opera star).

Belsom's third important New Orleans singer would be "Sydney Raynor, a tenor in the thirties and forties."

Marguerite Piazza "sang at the Met, but she made her career with nightclub appearances," Belsom said. Xavier-trained singers Debria Brown, Annabelle Bernard, and Gail Gilmore all had success on stage. Loyola's Harry Theyard sang at the Metropolitan Opera, as did soprano Angela Mannino, also trained at Loyola.

Sarah Jane McMahon, Elizabeth Futral, and Jeanne-Michelle Charbonnet all have appeared in New Orleans recently. Greer Grimsley, bass-baritone, has an international career and sings at the Met.

Fans of *Boardwalk Empire*, the HBO series about 1920s Atlantic City, can admire the acting ability of New Orleans native Anthony Laciura, playing the role of Eddie Kessler. Laciura, a tenor, honed his acting skills on the operatic stage. His first performance, as a child, was with Norman Treigle in a New Orleans production of the opera *Louise*. With degrees from Tulane and Loyola, Laciura went on stage at the Metropolitan Opera in New York for some eight hundred performances. Laciura's last performance in New Orleans was in October 2011, in the role of the Emperor Altoum in *Turandot*.

Wherever New Orleans singers go, they usually come home, as when many singers gathered at Loyola to honor Frohnmayer and his fellow teacher and wife, Ellen, in 2011. Perhaps the applause from your home audience is always the sweetest?

The Dancing Preisser Sisters

I KNEW NOTHING about the Preisser Sisters, a Ziegfeld Follies dance act from New Orleans, until I was working on my master's thesis at the University of New Orleans. My topic was Harry Hopkins, famed for his Depression-era work with the Works Progress Administration. Hopkins spent World War I with the American Red Cross in New Orleans. I was surprised to learn that his Chicago-based son, David, had married Orleanian Cherry Preisser, one of the dancing sisters, and that their daughter, Dr. June Hopkins, was a historian. Dr. Hopkins was very helpful, and we corresponded.

Then, while I was having lunch and watching television one afternoon in February 2003, Turner Classic Movies ran a brief black and white film entitled *Wash My Steps*. Billed as part of TCM's Festival of Shorts, the 1930s-era movie chronicled the adventures of a washing machine salesman who peddled his wares by tap-dancing with housewives. The young man soon became amorously involved with one of two tap-dancing sisters—whose father happened to own a rival washing machine company. All ended well, terpsichorically speaking. Surprisingly, this was perhaps the only performance caught on film of the brunette, Cherry Preisser, in the New Orleans dancing sisters duet that went from Ziegfeld to Hollywood.

I notified June Hopkins and I e-mailed Turner Classic Movies. Happily, they responded by sending a video of *Wash My Steps*. Dr. Hopkins told me that watching the video was the first time she and her siblings had ever seen their mother dance.

Cherry Blossom Preisser and her sister, June, were both pretty girls, one (June) blonde and one (Cherry) brunette. They were cheerful and energetic dancers in the Ruby Keeler style, but with a lot of acrobatics—flips and handstands and splits galore. Their father was Frederick Preisser, and their mother was Victorine Landrieu (who

Cherry and June Preisser. Photo courtesy of June Hopkins, Ph.D.

was former New Orleans Mayor Moon Landrieu's first cousin) and they grew up in New Orleans with their four brothers: Frederick, Thomas, Victor, and Ulrich. The girls were not the only local notables—brother Fred lettered in football at Tulane University in 1934, 1935, and 1936 and played in the very first Sugar Bowl game in 1935 (Tulane beat Temple University 20–14).

June, the blonde sister, was the younger one, and in her Hollywood career she appeared in numerous films—with Mickey Rooney in two Andy Hardy movies and *Strike up the Band* and in a string of 1940s college movies as coed Dodie Rogers.

According to an interview given to the *Roosevelt Review* (a New Orleans hotel magazine) June and Cherry both took dancing lessons as youngsters and through an uncle they met Orleanian Ted Liuzza, who was in the entertainment business. Appearances at church and neighborhood functions followed. June said that an Orpheum talent manager saw her doing cartwheels in her front yard on Wuerpel Street in Gentilly, and the sisters went on the Orpheum Vaudeville Circuit.

In a 1938 story, the *Times-Picayune* quoted June as saying, "I never did take tapping, I just picked it up." A 1937 story on Cherry Preisser in the *Times-Picayune* credited the sisters with beginning their public careers by dancing to entertain victims of the 1927 flood.

The girls owed their success as much to their personalities as to their talent. As June said in 1938, "Tap dancing is easy, and if you have charm and personality, they don't even look to see what your feet are doing."

The girls appeared in the Ziegfeld Follies of 1934 and were signed again two years later. The 1936 Follies was a classic. This time, besides Cherry and June, there was another young sibling act on the bill, the Nicholas Brothers. Star Fannie Brice was making her last appearance in a Ziegfeld show, and Bob Hope, Josephine Baker (returning to America after her triumphs in Paris), and Eve Arden were also in the cast. Music was by Ira Gershwin. George Balanchine was making his Broadway debut as a choreographer but perhaps made no suggestions to the Preissers or the Nicholases. The show was a success, in spite of the unusually high ticket price of $5.50.

The sister act would break up the next year when it was revealed in July that Cherry Preisser and David Hopkins, son of President Franklin D. Roosevelt's trusted advisor Harry Hopkins and his first wife, Ethel Gross, had secretly wed in Gretna, Louisiana, on June 22, 1937.

According to their daughter, it was a true love match. "Although neither Harry Hopkins nor Ethel Hopkins (divorced since 1931) were very happy about the match, both of them came to, first, accept Cherry as a daughter-in-law, and then love her. It would have been pretty hard not to. . . ."

David Hopkins, according to his daughter, was a "stage door Johnny" who was a student at the University of Chicago when he spied Cherry dancing in the Ziegfeld Follies tour. Not surprisingly, the story about a New Deal figure's son marrying a dancer was big news. Conservative columnist Westbrook Pegler was especially critical of the young couple.

David and Cherry had more in common than people knew—New Orleans itself. As a child of four, David had moved with his parents from New York to New Orleans, and lived in the city while Harry Hopkins worked for the Red Cross.

Cherry continued dancing for a few years after the wedding, according to June, and "when the war broke out, Daddy joined the navy and fought in the Pacific, on an aircraft carrier. Mother took my older sister and me to Southern California and she stopped dancing."

Following World War II, David Hopkins went into the movie business, and his company, Enterprise Studios, produced the movie *The Arch of Triumph*. Hopkins later began a career in advertising and with his family, which included six daughters by then, moved from California to Mamaroneck, New York, in 1952. A move back to Hollywood would follow. A son, Harry, was born in 1956 and another daughter in 1959, making a total of eight Hopkins children in all.

June Hopkins said that her father, who remained with McCann Erickson/Interpublic advertising agency, was transferred to Sydney, Australia, in 1963. The two oldest daughters did not make the trip—June was married and Cherry was working for *Vogue* magazine.

The first of the dancing Preissers to leave the stage was Cherry. "Mother died in 1964 of cancer and Daddy died in 1980. He had remarried after Mother died and had two more children," June Hopkins said.

June Preisser continued as a solo entertainer, operated dance schools, and married a radio personality, Dick Terry. They had one son, Josiah Moss "Ricky" Terry, who was killed in a car wreck with his mother in 1984.

None of the Preisser sisters' offspring have become dancers. According to June, "All of us girls took ballet lessons as children but were woefully untalented—Mother never seemed to care. She never danced again, never talked much about her career. We never really knew just how good she was."

The Jazz Magnet

New Orleans has long been a magnet to musicians.

A Swede, a Briton, and a onetime New Yorker—Lars Edegran, Clive Wilson, and Bruce Raeburn—have all brought their considerable talents to New Orleans, and traditional jazz is the better for their efforts.

"I did not come here first, you know, I went to Chicago," explained musician Lars Edegran. The Swedish Edegran was a blues fan, and at a blues concert in Germany he went backstage, where he met a Chicago record store owner who offered him a job if he decided to go to America.

"I saved up my money, bought a ticket, flew to New York in 1965 and took a Greyhound bus to Chicago," Edegran said, recalling his reaction to arriving in a snowstorm. "My God! Did I leave Sweden to come to this? It was worse than Stockholm."

Chicago presented a unique problem. "I couldn't go to the jazz clubs because I was underage, I was only twenty. That was a real drag," he admitted. He hitchhiked to New Orleans.

Edegran first went to Preservation Hall, where a group of musicians were rehearsing. "I got invited in by Allan Jaffe [the hall's proprietor]. I explained I played piano and he let me sit in with the band." Edegran met more traditional jazz musicians at Buster's Restaurant on Burgundy Street. He quit his Chicago job.

Soon he was part of a group of young musicians in town to learn the music. The group would ultimately include, among many others, Orjan "Orange" Kellin of Sweden, John Simmons, Barry Martyn, and Clive Wilson, all of England, and Tom Sancton, who chronicled his adventures in *Song for My Fathers* (Other Press, 2006).

Edegran, besides piano, also played clarinet and guitar in small dance halls, including Munster's, uptown at Laurel and Lyons Street,

Bruce Raeburn at the Hogan Jazz Archive. Photo by Carolyn Kolb.

and Luthjen's, downtown on Marais at Almonaster, with Sharkey Bonano's band, and at clubs on Bourbon Street. He even had a part-time job at the Hogan Jazz Archive at Tulane University and there he made an interesting discovery: a cache of musical arrangements of ragtime-era bandleader John Robichaux. From that grew the New Orleans Ragtime Orchestra. "We played at the Newport Jazz Festival, we did tours," he explained. The 1978 movie *Pretty Baby* used the ragtime orchestra on the soundtrack, which received an Oscar nomination.

Edegran's friend Vernel Bagneris asked him to work on the music for a re-creation of a black 1920s-era vaudeville show, and thus began a long association with *One Mo' Time*. "We were in New York for five years, we traveled. When we were in England we played for the queen," and there he met Kathy, his wife of twenty-three years. Today he is still in New Orleans and he still plays music. "Every week is different. But I can't complain for lack of work, there's plenty of work," he added.

Trumpeter Clive Wilson was the son of a Church of England clergyman in London and was a physics student at Newcastle University when the recordings of trumpeter Bunk Johnson and clarinetist George Lewis galvanized his desire to go to New Orleans.

Arriving in the summer of 1964, Wilson obtained a green card, so he could legally work to help pay for his trip. "I had the most incredible visit, making a hundred new friends in a matter of weeks. They all helped out, by finding me a place to stay, finding me a job, and of course inviting me to come to jam sessions at Preservation Hall," Wilson recalled fondly. "There was this wonderful experience of becoming part of the New Orleans culture—very different in the 1960s from Great Britain."

Civil rights legislation allowed white musicians to not only play with African American musicians but to join their musicians' union. "My experience, without knowing it at the time, was that I had found a new family—it was that personal," Wilson asserted.

After a time back in Britain, Wilson found a day job as a computer programmer at the First National Bank of Commerce. Luckily he didn't need it long. He and his Monette trumpet have stayed busy playing and recording. He formed a band, the Original Camellia Jazz Band, named for a 1920s group, and another group called the New Orleans Serenaders.

Wilson, like most of the young musicians who came here to learn, is now an American citizen. Post-Katrina New Orleans still offers him opportunities: "Now more than ever they expect music for everything: when the Natchez returned, when the port had a ceremony, when the Riverwalk reopened, they hired music. This is what people in New Orleans do, and it's unique, really in the world," Wilson said. "There is more support for live music in this relatively small city than just about anywhere."

Since 1989, Bruce Raeburn has been curator of the Hogan Jazz Archive at Tulane University, information headquarters for traditional New Orleans jazz. Raeburn points out that the passion of young European musicians in the 1960s was an outgrowth of the revival of interest in traditional New Orleans jazz that first came to prominence in the 1940s. European interest in traditional jazz and the blues was also a reflection of the politics of the left, and Raeburn noted that the same impulse that brought musicians to New Orleans would lead English music stars like Eric Clapton to study the blues.

Raeburn was the New York–born son of a jazz singer mother and a big band leader father, Boyd Raeburn, who began in the 1930s with swing and "by 1944 probably had the first white band to be influential in the impact of bebop on big bands." The band dissolved, the family moved to the Bahamas where his mother died, and Raeburn and his sister went to live with an uncle in California where he spent a freshman year of college at U.C.L.A. By 1966 his father had remarried and moved to Lafayette, and after his father's death Raeburn completed college as a history major at what is now the University of Louisiana at Lafayette, where he also earned a master's in history. In Lafayette, he also picked up drumsticks.

Raeburn arrived in New Orleans in 1971 as a history graduate student at Tulane, ultimately earning his Ph.D. with a dissertation on "the awakening of jazz scholarship and the effect those ideas had on New Orleans jazz." Studying was a day job, but at night Raeburn worked as a drummer. His gigs included a stint with James Booker ("Booker had two drummers: he called us 'the Angola Candidates'"), as a regular performer at the Maple Leaf, and ultimately with his own rock band Shot Down in Ecuador, Junior.

Raeburn marvels at the kindness of the New Orleans music world and at the overlapping types of music it holds. "The innate generosity of it—after having to deal with racial oppression for a long time, these black musicians were willing to take in these young white students," he noted.

"Even though I'm an outsider I have managed to end up on stage with some interesting local people—which is the dream of every outsider." In New Orleans, Raeburn insists, "it is possible to be a New Orleans person even if you weren't born here."

"Doc" Souchon

When you hear the gravelly recorded voice of Edmond "Doc" Souchon singing "If Ever I Cease to Love," the Mardi Gras anthem, you can tell it comes from the heart, and you can readily believe that the happiest man in New Orleans on Carnival Day, 1949, was most likely that singer.

Souchon's daughter Dolly Ann was reigning that year as Queen of Carnival, and the foremost practitioner of the music he loved best was reigning as King of Zulu: Louis Armstrong. Life doesn't get much better than that for a jazz fanatic who was willing to get up at dawn for Zulu and stay up past the Meeting of the Courts at midnight.

Edmond Souchon was born in New Orleans on October 25, 1897—his father, also a physician, played guitar and French horn, and his mother played the piano. Edmond, or "Doc" as he was known, grew up in the city, went to Tulane, became a physician and practiced medicine, but he gave his heart to jazz, managing to play and record and write about the music he loved. His record and book collections found their way to both the New Orleans Public Library and to the Louisiana State Museum, which absorbed the collection of the New Orleans Jazz Museum, a project of the New Orleans Jazz Club, of which Doc was an avid member. Until his death in 1969, he was a staunch supporter of the revival of interest in traditional New Orleans jazz.

The New Orleans that Souchon grew up in was, in many ways, a small town. He remembered hearing Joe "King" Oliver play—his baby nurse brought him along to "second line" funerals that passed near his St. Charles Avenue neighborhood. Music was played in his home, and his grandmother gave him his first guitar—but his interest piqued only when he heard a small ragtime combo at a ballroom dancing class.

Edmond "Doc" Souchon. Photo courtesy of Louisiana Division/City Archives, New Orleans Public Library.

Always adventuresome when it came to music, Souchon was willing to visit any neighborhood in search of good sounds, and his good memory made him a useful interview subject for later researchers. Besides following bands to clubs, Souchon danced to small jazz groups at parties in homes, and when he was a student at Tulane, larger bands played for dances. He firmly believed that New Orleans jazz deserved to be danced to, that the musicians expected their audience to participate in the music, not just sit and listen. Predictably, the background music in Souchon's life was always jazz—even his wife, Marie Estoup, played piano and could "rag" a tune.

In an oral history interview done by Haywood Hillyer III, in 1958, Souchon noted that he "had gotten more pleasure from jazz than anyone could dream." He prided himself on being the sole native Orleanian who began serious research into jazz history when interest in the early music was revived in the mid-twentieth century. "It has been a lonesome one-man stand," he mused.

When he was a teenager, Souchon, using the guitar his grandmother had given him, began playing music himself. He would play with fellow Orleanians vacationing in Pass Christian. Back in New Orleans, he and his friends formed a group called the Six and

Seven/Eighths String Band, and began playing for social occasions—a highlight was their gig for the Queen of Carnival's Supper Dance in 1912. The band got its name because of the height of violinist Hilton "Midget" Harrison in its original membership. Besides Souchon, on guitar and banjo, and Harrison, those in the original group included Charles Hardy on ukulele, Bill Gibbons on guitar, Shields O'Reardon on mandolin, Earl Crumb on drums or banjo, and Bob Reynolds on guitar.

By the 1950s, when the Six and Seven/Eighths String Band recorded, Souchon was still playing but was joined by Bill Kleppinger on mandolin, Frank "Red" Mackie on bass, and Bernie Shields on steel guitar. Folkways released the record, with versions of "When the Saints Go Marching In" and "Tiger Rag" among the standards on the disc.

On other discs, Souchon recorded with both white and African American musicians—including Danny and Blue Lu Barker, Raymond Burke, Monk Hazel, Paul Barbarin, Paul Burke, Jeanette Kimball, Johnny St. Cyr, Chink Martin, Sherwood Mangiapane, Armand Hug, Harry Shields, Mike Lala, Jack Delaney, and Pinky Vidacovich.

The other great love of Souchon's life was Carnival, especially the Rex organization. As a hobby, he created intricate miniature Rex floats, even making tiny marching bands by painting toy soldiers and giving them miniature instruments, his grandson John Parker recalled. The Mardi Gras floats were displayed at one time in the Rex Room at Antoine's, and are now treasured by his granddaughter C. C. Langenstein (Mrs. William), and some are said to be in the collection of the Louisiana State Museum.

Souchon wrote songs: "Deacon, Deacon, Deacon," a novelty tune, was penned with his friend, fellow guitarist Percy McKay, whose day job was in the hierarchy of the Whitney Bank. As usual, love of traditional jazz in New Orleans encompassed all strata of society. In one other creative endeavor, Souchon coauthored a book with fellow jazz enthusiast Al Rose. *New Orleans Jazz: A Family Album* contains pictures and biographical data on a host of New Orleans musicians, and on the places where they played and the bands they played in. The book was an immediate hit with both serious jazz fans and sentimental Orleanians.

Souchon and his music are not forgotten today. His voice still rings over the airways at Carnival with "If Ever I Cease to Love," and his grandson John Parker is a professional musician.

Early on, John mentioned to his grandfather that he was interested in music. As John recalled, "Fortunately, he challenged me: if you show that you're serious with it, I'll give you a guitar . . . that was a big deal for me when he gave me that guitar." Souchon suggested he take lessons at Guy Filiberto's guitar studio. "I guess I did get some foundation there," John admitted. Luckily, Doc's grandson was talented and worked hard. Later on, John received a Steinway piano that had belonged to his grandmother, which was sadly lost in Hurricane Katrina. Also lost in the flood were Souchon's tenor banjo and John's first guitar. "But I still have an old Martin guitar and a six-string banjo that belonged to him," John added.

Souchon died when his grandson was "just shy of fourteen," John remembered. "I had just started playing." Besides being Orleanians, grandfather and grandson had some things in common: "I'm kind of like my grandfather; I don't have the technical expertise, but, like him, I love to play the music," John admitted, modestly.

"I play solo, and I play with small and large jazz bands," John Parker noted. "I'm a sideman sometimes, and a band leader other times." While he plays "just guitar and banjo in public," John is also at home at the piano. Obviously there's a little bit of rhythm in that Souchon blood.

"Doc" Souchon would be proud that his descendant is helping keep alive the music, and the city, he loved so much. You might say he has his own generational "second line."

Piano Bars

THERE IS SOMETHING SPECIAL about a piano bar. First, as music historian Jack Stewart notes, the piano really gets the patron's attention. "The piano is the entertainment—they turn off the television."

New Orleans has always been a good town for piano bars (several are available today, including the revolving Carousel Bar at the Monteleone Hotel, where Stewart spent a recent evening). "Tuts" Washington at the Pontchartrain Hotel, "Cousin Joe" (Pleasant Joseph) at Poodle's Patio—the piano entertainers of the past left their mark on New Orleans memories. In fact, if you want to track sites of jazz history, check out Stewart's jazz walking tours for the New Orleans Jazz National Historical Park at http://www.nps.gov/jazz/history culture/places.htm.

Piano entertainers past and present all provide different takes on entertaining as a single. One of the best-known jazz pianists of the past was Armand Hug. Even Hug's 1977 funeral was "a quiet kind of thing," according to his sister-in-law Lee Baker. "That's the way his music was. He'd play all kinds of things, but he always played them quiet."

Armand Hug played mainly in a traditional New Orleans jazz style, but he had ragtime in his repertoire, a wide range of popular tunes he remembered, and a fondness for jazz a little outside his usual zone.

Hug could read music, but was mainly adept at "faking it." Once he had a job at the Suburban Gardens in Johnny Dedroit's band. The band was supposed to play "The Mexican Hat Dance"—always a New Orleans favorite—but Hug had trouble keeping up with the sheet music. Dedroit was not pleased and admitted he didn't like "fakers." On the next number, however, a girl singer wanted to sing "Who's

Charles Farmer at the piano at the Oak Street Café, 8140 Oak Street. Photo by Carolyn Kolb.

Sorry Now" but had no music with her. Armand took over, and Dedroit had to admit that the ability to fake could be useful.

In the 1940s Hug began his career as a solo performer, playing clubs and hotel night spots. He was a fixture at the Royal Orleans, in the St. Louis Street lobby in an area called the Esplanade Room. Even when arthritis stiffened his fingers, he had treatments, exercised, and went on playing—even earning an award from the Arthritis Foundation for his determination.

In a 1965 interview with jazz writer Charles Suhor, Armand Hug said, "Playing ragtime and Dixieland does not give you the full scope that you would really like to have. It doesn't give you the real, full freedom of improvisation." And playing solo piano would give an adventurous musician a lot of room to experiment.

Playing solo piano can also be an economic necessity, according to

Ellis Marsalis, renowned music educator and head of one of New Orleans's best-known musical families.

Marsalis started on the clarinet and then went to tenor saxophone and ended up on the piano—which proved rewarding since work was often available for a solo performer.

A nightclub might have a bandstand piano not used during the week, so a piano player might find week-night work. Or the establishment might have only enough room for a piano.

Marsalis brought his unique jazz piano style to the Hyatt Hotel for several years. "I was doing double duty. I would play for 'Happy Hour' in the atrium and sometimes there would be a band that would come in town that would use me, too. So, they didn't have to bring a piano player with them because I was already here. They'd save on salary as well as transportation." And, this gave Marsalis a chance to play with a wide range of groups. "You have to have a particular kind of mindset in order for it to work—not everybody is willing to make the adjustments to play with different people."

Playing solo piano is a special skill. "If you just play piano you have all of the responsibility—melody, solo, the rhythms—you're like a one-person orchestra," Marsalis explained. Some piano players sing—Marsalis does so only occasionally. And he is modest about his showmanship: "Sometimes I make an attempt to say something that turns out to be funny. But I don't have a schematic approach to being funny."

He prefers a grand piano to an upright: "Invariably it's up against the wall so that your back is to a lot of people." A grand piano, while good for audience interaction, can pose its own problems. At Snug Harbor one zealous female fan actually crawled under Marsalis's piano and led the club manager on a chase around the stage before she finally exited.

Marsalis has a jazz group now performing at Snug Harbor on Friday nights (at 8 and 10 o'clock.) His band work and his solo work have been two intertwined parts of his musical career, along with his teaching (at the New Orleans Center for Creative Arts and at the University of New Orleans).

Marsalis has proudly sought his own musical truth: "You have to play in such a way that you allow your audience to find you. It may take a while. It usually does. But the main thing is to be as honest as you can be when you are playing."

In the past, the piano itself was the entertainment center of the home. "Now it's a four-hundred-pound instrument that nobody plays. You can get them for free," according to Charles Farmer, who grew up in Oklahoma but now makes his home here, and repairs pianos as well as playing them.

When he isn't repairing instruments, Farmer has a regular piano gig—he plays from 9:30 a.m. to 1:30 p.m. at the Oak Street Café, most days of the week except Tuesday. You can have breakfast and enjoy his music (Ellis Marsalis drops in occasionally). He also moonlights with a group, and composes: his latest project is a string quartet.

Farmer's repertoire is eclectic—spending eighteen years in Greece gave him familiarity with European tourist tastes. He likes rhythm and blues, knows traditional jazz tunes ("Do You Know What It Means to Miss New Orleans" is his most requested song), and even can do country. Since he was born in Tulsa, "that's required," and he even knows some of legendary country swing bandleader Bob Wills's songs. "But I don't play 'Take Me Back to Tulsa,' 'cause I don't want to go, except to see my mom," Farmer explained.

The Oak Street Café job came up after Hurricane Katrina when Farmer was looking for something to tide him over until he could find nighttime work. Farmer enjoys his daytime venue, and recognizes that it is different from the usual job. "There's no alcohol. There are older people, and people with young children. I meet people there that I wouldn't on a regular gig," he said.

And there is that special effect of having a piano player in the room. "People come and sit by me. Sometimes there are rather surprisingly personal conversations," Famer admits. "And, if I do the job correctly, there's a feeling of intimacy and relaxation."

All the more reason to respect the keyboard artists who have entertained Orleanians through the years.

Music Bibliography

It's obvious. If you want to know about New Orleans music, you're going to have to listen to it. How? In the age of the Internet, that's—as they say—a no-brainer.

Go to www.wwoz.org.

You can listen online to this public radio station that dedicates its airtime to showcasing New Orleans music. Weekdays around 9 a.m. central time you can hear some traditional jazz. Evenings you might catch a rhythm and blues show. The on-air voices are volunteers, musicians actually show up and play, and the station broadcasts from a booth at the New Orleans Fairgrounds during the annual Jazz and Heritage Festival (www.nojazzfest.com) the last weekend of April and first weekend of May.

And, if you like New Orleans music, you have to make a pilgrimage to the Jazz Festival at least once in your lifetime. (Of course, you can hear live music all the time: WWOZ broadcasts a list of who is playing where in town on every uneven hour.)

Online Resources

WWOZ can give you information on artists' recordings available, and here are two websites for New Orleans music retailers: Louisiana Music Factory has a little bit of everything, and Jazzology focuses on traditional jazz.

www.Jazzology.com
www.louisianamusicfactory.com

Sometimes just trolling around the Internet will yield some musical gems. Here are some suggestions:

Kermit Ruffins, trumpeter, is a consummate entertainer. I love his rendition of "Happy Birthday to You" because he sings the verse "You look like a monkey and you smell like one, too" that always makes me laugh. Go to www.youtube.com for this one. Send it to your nearest and dearest on their day.

Royes Fernandez was one of New Orleans's greatest gifts to ballet. You will agree after watching him partner Maria Tallchief in a pas de deux from *Les Sylphides*. Go to www.youtube.com (Even in grainy black and white, not only are they lovely dancers individually; together they are magical.)

This incredibly raunchy music video has to be seen to be believed: it was shot in a Walmart, and the music is "bounce." YouTube doesn't have it anymore—Google "Mr. Ghetto" + "WalMart" + Bounce + "Music Video." New Orleans musicians are creative, to say the least.

Video

The HBO series *Tremé* has beautifully incorporated New Orleans music and musicians into its storyline. Watch it first run, or you can get a DVD to watch the first season at your leisure.

Tremé: The Complete First Season. 2011. HBO Home Video.

Books

For basic information about the very early music scene in New Orleans, Dr. Henry A. Kmen's book is essential. He was a musician himself and played on board the steamer *President* with the Crawford-Ferguson Night Owls in the 1960s. The full text of this book is available from JStor, an online service most university libraries provide.

Kmen, Henry A. 1966. *Music in New Orleans: The Formative Years, 1791–1841*. Baton Rouge, La.: Louisiana State University Press.

The musicians themselves not only make the music; they live it. Louis Armstrong's book comes from his own writings—the language may have been somewhat altered, and this might be a sanitized version of life on the streets of New Orleans at the start of the twentieth century, but this is a saga of an artist coming into his own. Allen Lomax tells the complex story of Jelly Roll Morton, and a real person comes through. Mac Rebennack and his alter ego, "Dr. John," take the New Orleans music scene further along into perhaps a tougher and less forgiving time.

Armstrong, Louis. 1954. *Satchmo: My Life in New Orleans*. New York: Prentice-Hall Books.

Lomax, Allen. 1950; 2001. *Mister Jelly Roll: The Fortunes of Jelly Roll Morton, New Orleans Creole and "Inventor of Jazz."* Berkeley, Ca.: University of California Press.

Rebennack, Mac, with Jack Rummel. 1994. *Under a Hoodoo Moon: The Life of Dr. John the Night Tripper*. New York: St. Martin's Press.

These three books deal with the early years of jazz and the musicians who created it, and with New Orleans as the spot where that creation happened. The Rose/Souchon book is a handy, if incomplete, directory of New Orleans musicians. The Shapiro/Hentoff book is a standard overview that uses musicians' own words and places the city and the music in a wider context. Raeburn, who is curator of the Hogan Jazz Archive at Tulane University, takes a scholarly look at how jazz historians and critics over the years have dealt with the city as the place where the music first emerged.

Rose, Al, and Dr. Edmond Souchon. 1967; 2001. *New Orleans Jazz: A Family Album*. Baton Rouge, La.: Louisiana State University Press.

Shapiro, Nat, and Nat Hentoff, eds. 1966. *Hear Me Talkin' to Ya: The Story of Jazz by the Men Who Made It*. New York: Dover Publications.

Raeburn, Bruce. 2009. *New Orleans Style and the Writing of American Jazz History*. Ann Arbor, Mich.: University of Michigan Press.

New Orleans not only gave birth to jazz; the city also nurtured the growth of rhythm and blues, a musical genre on its own and also a predecessor of rock and roll. These books will tell that story and introduce you to the musicians who made it happen.

Broven, John. 1978. *Rhythm and Blues in New Orleans* (original title *Walking to New Orleans: The Story of New Orleans R & B*). New Orleans: Pelican Publishing Company.

Hannusch, Jeff. 1985. *I Hear You Knockin': The Sound of New Orleans Rhythm and Blues.* Ville Platte, La.: Swallow Publications.
Berry, Jason, with Jonathan Foose and Tad Jones. 1986; 2009. *Up from the Cradle of Jazz: New Orleans Music Since World War II.* Lafayette, La.: University of Louisiana at Lafayette Press.

The New Orleans music scene today is vibrant and eclectic. You can hear a little bit of everything on the streets, in the clubs, on WWOZ, and at various festivals. These two books will give you a contemporary take on local sounds and artists. (10th Ward Buck is also Mr. Ghetto, the producer of the Walmart video.)

Fensterstock, Allison, and 10th Ward Buck. 2011. *The Definition of Bounce: Between Ups and Downs in New Orleans.* New Orleans: Garrett County Press.
Swenson, John. 2011. *New Atlantis: Musicians Battle for the Survival of New Orleans.* New York: Oxford University Press.

You can't really know New Orleans music until you experience Ernie K-Doe, even if only in the pages of a book. Trust me on this one.

Sandmel, Ben. 2012. *Ernie K-Doe: The R&B Emperor of New Orleans.* New Orleans: Historic New Orleans Collection.

Recorded Music

The best New Orleans recordings? Well, we are all going to have different opinions on that, aren't we? I am going to list recordings I like, but I would suggest that you find an artist or group, sample something they did by listening to them online, and then check the Louisiana Music Factory or Jazzology websites if you can't find them easily. And, if hip-hop or rap or bounce is what you crave, New Orleans has a wide range of top artists, and new ones are making their way on to the scene every day.

Traditional jazz was not just performed in halls and at concerts; it was still used as a folk music, for parades, funerals, dance halls, up into the 1960s. Everyone from a shoeshine boy to the Eureka Brass Band, from Billie and

DeDe Pierce to Champion Jack Dupree to Roosevelt Sykes and even Edmond "Doc" Souchon and the Six and Seven/Eighths String Band—the Smithsonian Institution captured New Orleans jazz, blues, and gospel in the mid-twentieth century.

Various artists, 1951–1961. *Classic Sounds of New Orleans*. Smithsonian Folkways.

The marching bands of New Orleans played military and religious music, but with their own beat. The Eureka re-creates a funeral, and Bunk Johnson—who had been out of music for several decades—has a real sound of the past in this rough 1945 recording.

Eureka Brass Band. 1992 (recorded 1951). *New Orleans Funeral & Parade: The Original 1951 Session*. American Music Records.

Bunk Johnson. 1994 (recorded 1945). *Bunk's Brass Band and Dance Band 1945*. American Music Records.

The quintessential ingredients for the New Orleans sound can be found in these three piano players. Professor Longhair has his signature beat, Fats Domino rocks it out, and Allen Toussaint is a genius at composing standards. (And he is still at it!)

Professor Longhair. 1990 (original release 1972). *New Orleans Piano*. Atlantic Records.

Fats Domino. 2007. *Greatest Hits: Walking to New Orleans*. Capitol Records.

Allen Toussaint. 2011. *Everything I Do Gonh Be Funky: The Hit Songs & Productions, 1957–1978*. Snapper Records, U.K.

Many New Orleans musicians had relatives in the business, but the outstanding musical families of today are the Nevilles and the Marsalis clan. The Neville Brothers (Art, Charles, Aaron, and Cyril) also encompassed the Meters (Art and Cyril were members of that group, along with George Porter, Jr., Leo Nocentelli, and David Russell Batiste, Jr.). This recording of the Marsalis family (father Ellis on piano, Branford on sax, Delfeayo on trombone, Jason on drums, and Wynton on trumpet) even includes Ellis III, a poet, and their longtime family friend Harry Connick, Jr., on piano.

The Meters. 1997. *The Very Best of the Meters*. Rhino Records.
Neville Brothers. 2004. *20th Century Masters—Millennium Collection: The Best of the Neville Brothers*. A & M Records.
Marsalis Family. 2010. *Music Redeems*. Marsalis Music.

These three performers represent the New Orleans sound to the world. Connick and Rebennack have careers mainly outside the city, but Irma Thomas is still a reigning queen of New Orleans music.

Harry Connick, Jr. 2011. *In Concert on Broadway: Harry Connick Jr.* Sony Records.
Mac Rebennack (Dr. John). 2008. *The Best of Dr. John: The Night Tripper*. Music Club Deluxe Records.
Irma Thomas. 2006. *After the Rain*. Rounder Records. (This was a Grammy winner.)

One of the most interesting modern reworkings of New Orleans music has been the change (could we call it funkification?) of the brass band. The Rebirth Brass Band won a well-deserved 2011 Grammy for this release.

Rebirth Brass Band. 2011. *Rebirth of New Orleans*. Basin Street Records.

Index

Page numbers in **bold** indicate illustrations.